Our Home In the Hills

True Stories About an Idyllic Ozark Childhood and
Treasured Family Recipes from the Last One Hundred Years

Marilyn Michel Whetstone

Inspiring Voices books may be ordered through booksellers or by contacting:

Inspiring Voices
1663 Liberty Drive
Bloomington, IN 47403
www.inspiringvoices.com
844-686-9605

Scriptures taken from the Holy Bible, New International Version®, NIV®.
Copyright © 1973, 1978, 1984, 2011 by Biblica, Inc.™ Used by permission
of Zondervan. All rights reserved worldwide. www.zondervan.com The
"NIV" and "New International Version" are trademarks registered in
the United States Patent and Trademark Office by Biblica, Inc.®

ISBN: 978-1-4624-1316-4 (sc)
ISBN: 978-1-4624-1317-1 (e)

Library of Congress Control Number: 2020920895

Print information available on the last page.

Inspiring Voices rev. date: 12/09/2020

"The author takes the reader back to a harder but better time. This book is a reminder of what is at risk today: abiding faith, marriages that are founded on 'until death do us part,' and the rewards that come from a strong work ethic.

Thank you to the author for a look back seventy years as well as for a heightened awareness of our need to be vigilant going forward."

—Jack Herschend, Silver Dollar City Founder

"Our Home in the Hills captures the history and culture of the Ozark hills. As a pastor and resident of Rockaway Beach, I am thankful for this resource to share with our community as we work in the same places that are detailed in this history."

—Jonathan McGuire, Pastor, Bridge of Faith Community Church

"Life then and now seems worlds apart, but the lessons are the same. People need to know what life was like only a few generations ago."

—Jeff Justus, Former Missouri Representative

To David, my biggest cheerleader

Contents

Introduction

"Mary, Mary! Ella fell in the well! Mary! Ella fell in the well!"

Mary, the oldest sister, in charge of the little ones while their parents made a trip into Branson for supplies, heard Lilly's scream for help from inside the small log cabin on a warm mid-April day in 1917. She came running toward the place where not-quite-three-year-old Ella and her siblings had been playing. Lilly, consumed with fear and anguish, shrieked in jerky sentences between sobs as she tried to explain that little Ella had tripped while close to the small well opening that was the source of the family's spring-fed drinking water. The well had been left uncovered accidentally, and Ella had lost her balance and fallen into a space that one would not believe was large enough for a child to slip through.

The fall was instantly fatal for little Ella—not due to drowning but because of a broken neck. Upon their return from town, Edwin and Ethel Rebecca Michel, parents of eight children, including three sets of twins at the time, learned of Ella's accident. They were devastated. Heartache and despair beyond what the human spirit seemed able to endure enveloped the grieving family, but as people have faced tragedy since the beginning of time, the Michels, through their deep faith in God, were somehow able to pick up the pieces of their brokenness and forge ahead.

The already large family eventually became even larger with a total of twelve children in the early years of the twentieth century.

They survived by perseverance, ingenuity, hard work, and God-given skills in the rugged hills of Taney County, Missouri.

Like the roots of a massive oak tree in this rocky soil bring moisture and nutrients to the tree itself, my roots are firmly established in the hills and hollers that have created rich traditions and culture in Ozark Mountain Country. I am a descendant of courageous pioneers who settled here and found harmony with this rugged land and its swift untamed waters. Hardship was an ever-present companion to the early settlers of our area, but family stories passed down illustrate that alongside hardship was the twin companion of the joy and comfort of a close-knit family. Like the strong, towering oak tree, family provides soothing water and rich nutrients to its own through all circumstances.

This is the story of my family. It is not a history book. It is a love story for my children, their children, and all who will come from them as their lives intertwine with past generations to deepen and enrich our family's story.

Daddy

In 1911, twins Vernie and Ernie were born to Edwin and Ethel (Pickett) Michel in McKinney Bend near Branson, Missouri—the family's second set of twins. Vernie, my father, was one of eleven children who grew to adulthood on ninety-six acres of rocky and hilly farmland near Branson. Mary, the oldest, was followed by the first set of twins, Willie and Lilly, then Charlie. After Charlie, Vernie and Ernie increased the size of the family to six children; they were followed three years later by twins Della and Ella. After Della and Ella, Ruth came along, then Exie and little sister Pearl. At the end of twenty years of childbearing, my grandmother gave birth to her last child, Edwin Lee. He rounded out the family of six girls and six boys, including three sets of twins: one set of boys, one set of girls, and a girl and boy.

Grandpa Edwin Benjamin Michel came from St. Louis with his parents when they acquired what became known as the Michel Homestead in McKinney Bend, just off what was originally known as Long Beach Road and later T Highway, about eight miles east of Branson. No money was exchanged for the ninety-six acres, but my great-grandparents—Berthold Jacob and Susan Michel, immigrants from Switzerland who originally settled in St. Louis and eventually in Branson nine years after immigrating to America—were able to take ownership by homesteading the land at the county seat in Forsyth. The story goes that they traded a blind mare and got two calves to boot for the beautiful rolling hills, streams, bottomland, and springs where the farm was established in 1885.

My father has told me that the boys and their dad would go into the fields after a heavy rain and dip water with a wash pan as a means of draining the field. Daddy (as my siblings and I called him) told us of the one cash product they produced: sorghum. They planted the cane in April and cultivated it precisely on September 1. On that day, they stripped the cane by taking off the blades and ran it through a sorghum mill. After that, they took the cane juice and cooked it with wood in an evaporator pan ten feet long and four feet wide. They would peddle this to neighbors to get cash to pay for necessities such as taxes, which usually amounted to about twenty dollars per year on their home and property. Everything else they grew or produced was used to sustain the large family.

Daddy was a great storyteller, and I learned much about his upbringing and his work ethic through his many, many tales about his parents and grandparents. I learned about their philosophy of life, and his, from his sayings and stories with a moral. From as long as I can remember, I was taught that "early to bed and early to rise makes a man healthy, wealthy, and wise." Another adage that has stayed with me throughout my life is, "You can catch more flies with honey than you can with vinegar." From his mother, Daddy passed down the saying, "You may not especially like your place in life, and I may not like mine, but I can think of thousands who would think our place was fine."

Daddy was not a parent who lectured his children, but he got his point across through his short sayings on how to live. One that he drilled into us (though, by his own admission, it was not original with him) was "Life is 10 percent what you make it and 90 percent how you take it." Books have been written on the power of a positive attitude, but Daddy summed it up in one sentence, and it has stayed with me always. Thanksgiving and gratitude for what one had were preached in his family's home, and Daddy reminded us daily of the importance of a grateful heart.

A child and young adult of the Great Depression era, Daddy related that his family had little money; they were able to support themselves and had what they needed but little extra. For example, he told how they would never consider hiding Easter eggs because they could not afford to lose even one egg to something as frivolous, from their perspective, as an Easter egg hunt. Being descendants of Baptist preachers, they understood the true meaning of Easter, and an Easter egg hunt was not part of that understanding.

Inside the log cabin on the Michel homestead was a single large main room; its focal point was the fireplace built with native fieldstone. Perhaps due to their Swiss ancestry, Grandpa Michel and all of his sons had a natural aptitude for carpentry, woodworking, and stone masonry. The family gradually added a loft and some additional rooms to the original log cabin. The children slept in the loft, where the boys had two nails on which to hang their two pairs of overalls, carefully separating their work or school overalls from their Sunday overalls.

After six days a week of diligent work on the farm to provide a living for the large family, Sunday was their day of rest. It included churchgoing, Sunday dinner, and time for being with family at home—playing games, hiking through the streams and hills, and learning to play musical instruments by ear, including guitar, banjo, piano, fiddle, and the intricately carved oak pump organ with a high back and round stool covered in red velvet. Since cash was scarce, trading and bartering were usually how instruments were acquired. In his early twenties, Daddy traded a cord of wood for his beautiful heirloom fiddle that is still in our family.

The Michels spent many a cold winter Sunday afternoon in front of the stone fireplace with their instruments, singing such old familiar hymns as "What a Friend We Have in Jesus" and folk songs as "She'll Be Coming Round the Mountain." One of Daddy's favorites that he strummed by ear on his fiddle and played by ear on the piano during my growing-up years was "The Tennessee Waltz."

Daddy had only an eleventh-grade education. He attended

Mountain Grove School in McKinney Bend until he completed eighth grade. There was no transportation to high school in Branson, so to attend, he and his brothers walked several miles north of the farm to the banks of Lake Taneycomo, where they took a rowboat about three miles around Long Beach Bend to the budding tourist destination known as Rockaway Beach. Once there, they tied the boat for the day and walked two blocks up the steep hill to New Flint Hill School, which was established in 1926. Daddy attended classes there through eleventh grade.

During his early high school years at New Flint Hill School, he and Ernie decided they wanted to earn some cash during their summer break, so they schemed together. Visionaries from an early age, they hatched the idea for a business and decided that the sidewalk in front of Captain Bill's Hotel, one of three very popular hotels on the beach, was the ideal location for their venture. Most of the streets were still unpaved and fairly dusty, and as sightseeing buses provided tours to various caves and to Shepherd of the Hills Country, the boys figured that city slickers' shoes were probably dusty at day's end. Could there be a need to offer a shoe-shining service to some of these well-heeled visitors? The boys figured they'd give it a try and find out.

For tourists, days filled with outdoor activities often ended at the dance pavilion along the shores of Lake Taneycomo, where the men dressed in their best Sunday suits and women donned high heels, long flowing cotton skirts, and snug-fitting blouses accentuating tiny waistlines to dance to live music through the evening hours. Although sixteen-year-old twins Vernie and Ernie only had overalls to wear, they set about establishing their shoe-shining business with a few old rags and a couple of round tins of brown and black shoe polish. However, one important part of the plan they forgot to consider was getting permission from Captain Bill to set it up on his property.

After silently observing the activities of the teenage boys for several days from his coffee shop window—where he sat drinking endless cups of hot coffee and supervising the friendly waitresses in their fresh starched white uniforms with a colorful hankie tucked in the bodice pocket—Captain Bill was impressed with the young boys' diligence and commitment to their venture and their friendliness and easy manner with the tourists. He approached them about their shoe-shining activity on his property. Tongue-tied and embarrassed by their negligence, they apologized and offered to close down. But he liked what he had observed and became convinced that his guests might like the service, so being a generous man with a big heart and an entrepreneurial spirit, he worked out an arrangement with the boys, and Vernie and Ernie began their business careers in Rockaway Beach with the blessing and support of Captain Bill.

Uncle Ernie eventually graduated from New Flint Hill High School, but Daddy dropped out at the end of the eleventh grade to return to the farm full-time and help sustain the large family. He never lived anywhere except the homestead until he married my mother at age twenty-eight. He did, however, continue to work summers in Rockaway at Captain Bill's Hotel in various roles. His outgoing personality, energy, and industrious nature were appreciated by Captain Bill Roberts, who eventually offered him full-time work at the hotel. It was never fully explained why Bill Roberts was given the title of Captain. He was not former military; he was, however, the manager of the extremely popular dance pavilion and the dance boat that navigated between Rockaway and Branson every evening. The pavilion hosted some of the most well-known live bands in the country. The bands, locals, and tourists would all board the dance boat and dance all the way down the nine-mile Lake Taneycomo trek to Branson and back, and then dance in the screened-in pavilion with its worn hardwood floors through the warm summer evenings.

It is possible that since Bill was the manager of the dance boat, he was dubbed with the nickname Captain. It stuck with him as he and his wife made their mark in Rockaway and contributed to its growth and prosperity through their property acquisitions, namely Captain Bill's Hotel and Restaurant. It was on this property that

Daddy began his lifelong love affair with the Beach. Eventually, he and my mother established their own business. He was coming of age as the area was entering its prime and evolving into what I like to think of as the golden era of Rockaway Beach.

Mother

On a Saturday night, with their instruments in tow, the Michel boys made their way just a few miles east of the farm to the small country frame home of their first cousin, Ruby Persinger, on a rolling hillside near Kirbyville. Once there, greetings were made, and the music began. Charlie had his banjo, Exie his guitar, and Vernie his fiddle. They sang and strummed songs like "This Land is Your Land" and "On the Sunny Side of the Street." With the week's work done, a lighthearted gaiety prevailed.

Among the party guests one night was a new face to some in the small Kirbyville community: Louise Reese, the dark-eyed, brown-haired, pretty young schoolteacher who had arrived in the fall of 1939 to teach in the grade-one-through-eight one-room country school. As was common in the day, one of the school families agreed to provide room and board for the teacher in their home during the school year. Fred and Ruby Persinger and their three young boys—Willard, Gordon, and Glenn—opened their home and their hearts to my mother and, of course, included her in the Saturday night birthday party festivities.

By this time, Vernie was working as a full-time employee of Captain Bill's Hotel. He was able to buy a few things for himself, and he showed up at the party in a spiffy new suit looking like "a Philadelphia lawyer," as I heard him say many times when describing a well-dressed gentleman. It was on this carefree autumn evening that twenty-eight-year-old Vernie met twenty-one-year-old Louise. With her dark brown eyes, slim figure, charm, and intelligence, he was smitten! He was also impressed with her educational achievements at such a young age.

As they began courting, she became equally impressed with his sense of humor, his sensitive heart, his devotion to his large family, and his values, which were compatible to her own. The large difference in their educational levels was insignificant to her. She always said that she knew he was "a good man," and one way she knew that was how he spoke of his mother and how he treated her with the greatest tenderness and respect.

Louise was born and raised in Brown Branch, Missouri. At the end of her eighth-grade year, she and her parents, Dow and Vera Reese, had to make a decision about her opportunities for high school. Like the farm in McKinney Bend, the small hamlet in far Eastern Taney County had no way to transport students to high school. The closest high schools to Brown Branch were in Ava, twenty miles to the east, and Forsyth, twenty miles to the west. The School of the Ozarks at Point Lookout, fifty miles away, offered boarding for students who were willing to leave their families after eighth grade to live and work on campus in return for their high school education.

My grandparents, affectionately called "Mom and Daddy Dow" by my siblings and me—and even further back, my great-grandparents, Albert and Eliza Dean—placed great value on education, so the decision was made that young Louise, barely thirteen years old, would go to the School of the Ozarks for high school. The institution was founded on the principal of earning one's education, and Mother was assigned the job of working in the canning factory once she arrived on campus. The number of hours students worked were limited because their schedules included, in addition to classes, sports and music. I never once heard Mother reflect on her years at S of O as being unpleasant or trying in any way, other than missing her family in Brown Branch. On the contrary, she loved her years there, and she was defined by a deep and fierce loyalty to the School of the Ozarks all of her life.

During my growing-up years, the homecoming, which always took place in November, was a highlight of our autumn months. Mother reunited with her high school friends, and there were activities including a barn dance, a basketball game, and plenty of food and fellowship to last for a fun-filled weekend. From her graduation in 1935 until her death in 1995, she never missed a homecoming at the school, and in her later years she became very involved in the alumni organization in leadership roles. In 1991, she was greatly honored to receive the Meritorious Award for Outstanding Service to the School of the Ozarks and the Branson Community.

After graduation from the School of the Ozarks in 1935, Mother, still wanting to pursue higher education, entered college. Mom and Daddy Dow, like so many of their fellow Americans, were emerging from the Great Depression and had four additional children at home. Undeterred by financial challenges, young Louise, along with her parents, worked out an arrangement with Mae Reese, a first cousin to Daddy Dow, who lived with her husband, Mr. Rhoads, in a large stately white-columned home in downtown Springfield, very close to the campus of Southwest Missouri State Teacher's College.

Cousin Mae, as she was referred to in our family until her death many, many years later, was a professional seamstress in Springfield. She worked with the finest materials and sewing notions available and with some of Springfield's ladies of high society. Mae offered to let Louise move in with her and Mr. Rhoads (as she called her own husband) if the young high school graduate was willing to do the housekeeping in the large home.

Mother seized what she viewed as a wonderful opportunity to be close to the campus with room and board provided, and somewhat flexible hours. Her dream of becoming a teacher just might be possible, and she had no intention of squandering the opportunity. She worked diligently at her studies and her housekeeping responsibilities and earned the admiration and respect of Cousin

Mae. After four years, she graduated with a degree in English and a certification to teach in Missouri public schools.

Her years with Cousin Mae exposed Mother to a level of sophistication she had not experienced in Brown Branch or in her years at S of O. She never became snobbish about it, but, as she observed, she learned new ways of doing things from Cousin Mae, and from Mae's circle of friends in Springfield. She learned how to properly set a beautiful table and entertain with fine crystal and silver tea sets. She gained a new appreciation for beautiful things and for creating a warm and inviting home environment, and she gained insight into how to conduct oneself in social settings with grace and, as she called it, "polish," a term she often used with my sisters and me.

During her first and only year of teaching school in 1939, a romance developed, and on September 7, 1940, Vernie and Louise were married at the First Presbyterian Church in the old town of Forsyth, Missouri, located on the banks of Swan Creek. Vernie and Louise—completely self-supporting and still practicing the frugality so familiar to them in their growing-up years—chose to keep the wedding simple. Louise wore a simple dark-colored day dress with long sleeves, a wide brimmed dark hat, and simple black pumps; she carried a black leather clutch bag and gloves. A lovely corsage of white flowers with sprigs of greenery cascaded gently over her left shoulder. Vernie wore a three-piece dark suit with white shirt and tie, a silk handkerchief neatly placed in his suit pocket—and, of course, perfectly shined dress shoes. Their wedding reception, appropriately, was held in the dining room of Captain Bill's Hotel, with its lodge-style checkered cloth table coverings, surrounded by their large families and wide circle of longtime friends from the Branson and McKinney Bend communities, Brown Branch, the School of the Ozarks, and even a few guests from Springfield and the teacher's college.

Married life for Mother and Daddy began on a few acres of heavily shaded, untamed land two blocks uphill from the shores of Lake Taneycomo, where tourists enjoyed a phenomenon of sorts for the central part of the country: Rockaway Beach, named after the one in New York by the Merriam family of Kansas City, whose brainchild it was. Tourists were impressed that they could find such an upscale resort area without having to travel to the beaches of the East Coast.

It was on this raw land that Daddy and Mother together built one little housekeeping cottage at a time. Each cottage was well constructed, many from native stone, and furnished on the inside with the comforts and amenities of home. The logo used on the leaf-shaped signs that my parents sprinkled along the main highway arteries into the Beach was, "Follow the Leaves to Your Home in the Hills." It was indeed a miniature home-away-from-home that Mother and Daddy strove to create for our guests on the patch of raw land they bought in 1940 and worked for more than forty-five years. They established a popular and beautiful summer resort that hosted up to 125 guests nightly in twenty-five cottages, with a lovely sprawling ranch-style home where many memories were woven into the tapestry of our lives.

New Flint Hill School

One time, two times, and yet a third time, we heard the large, inverted-cup-shaped cast-iron bell ringing loud and clear. Housed in the second floor belfry, it rang Monday through Friday to give a fifteen-minute warning that school was about to begin. Measuring two by three feet, the bell had a long scratchy rope that hung from the tower of the building to the first-floor porch of the school building, where it could be easily reached by adults and older children.

Miss Casey, the proverbial old-maid schoolteacher when I attended first, second, and third grade, made certain to tend to this daily chore to ensure the Beach children got to school on time. After all, she had to keep the schedule running punctually, because she had children ranging in age from five to fourteen to educate. Not an easy task, but she was an experienced one-room schoolteacher and accepted the call to teach in our grade-one-through-eight one-room school.

Karen, my cousin and dearest friend, and I were both just a few months past our fifth birthday when we entered first grade. Kindergarten was not part of the rural school curriculum at that time, and preschool was an unknown concept in rural southwest Missouri. Francine, my older sister, was in third grade at the time, and like most younger sisters, I wanted to do what my older sister did every day.

Uncle Lee, Daddy's youngest brother; his wife, Aunt Virginia; and Mother and Daddy met with Miss Casey, and it was determined that Karen and I would begin first grade in the fall of the 1950–51 school year. We joined two other first-graders, Buck and Gale. There were fifteen students in all being schooled in the large, well-kept room known as New Flint Hill School. We showed up every single day to begin our formal educational journey.

New Flint Hill was established in Rockaway in 1926. Prior to that, Flint Hill School, located at the intersection of Bull Creek and the White River, was established to educate the children of early-twentieth-century Rockaway Beach. In 1915, twenty-three students attended the one-room school—a hefty number for one teacher. The older students often assisted the teacher by teaching the younger students and supervising outdoor play. To escape the perils of flooding from the White River, Flint Hill School moved in 1926 about one mile east of where it had been and became New Flint Hill School.

A few hundred feet across the schoolyard in the little stone bungalow built by Daddy and Uncle Ernie in 1940, our day began early. Francie, Sherry, and I shared a double bed piled high with warm, cozy quilts. We were eager to go to school every day, so we only had to be called once by Daddy to "rise and shine." He made sure we awakened to a warm fire in the fireplace. Mother made sure we had a good breakfast, and off Francie and I trotted across the schoolyard to Miss Casey and our schoolmates as we heard the loud peals of the old reliable school bell.

It was a coveted privilege for the older children to be given the task of doing the ringing. The younger ones looked forward to when they might be big enough to pull the scratchy rope that could actually cause a burn on the palm of small hands struggling with the bell's enormous weight.

The schoolroom was warm and welcoming with its wall of windows spanning the length of the room. I loved peering out the paned-glass windows to the densely wooded forest that formed a backdrop to our schoolroom. During autumn days we watched the trees turn to shades of gold and red. During winter days we gazed at barren trees and bright blue skies or the occasional wintry snowfall, and I loved the fresh breeze and the scent of lilac and honeysuckle that filtered in through opened windows during springtime. The blackboard at the front of the room had trays for white chalk and erasers, and I was envious as a first-grader of the big kids who took turns during math bees. They went to the board eager to show their mathematical prowess and worked math problems that seemed to produce endless columns of numbers, and at the same time earn them the honor of being the contest winner of the day.

The hand-sawed and wide-planked hardwood floors always seemed to need sweeping, and there were tables for the younger children and several rows of adjoining desks with ink holes for the older ones. With our Big Chief tablets, pencils, and erasers, we had no need of an ink hole in the 1950s, but it was a carryover from previous decades and served as a useful little cubbyhole in which to prop our pencils and erasers for handy use.

The first thing Miss Casey did in the morning, after we said the pledge of allegiance, was to get us all started on our lessons—which, for first-graders, meant learning how to form letters and beginning the process of writing them independently. Each subject had a workbook, and as their predecessors did in Flint Hill School, the older children often helped the younger ones. Francie; Joan, our neighbor and favorite playmate; and Betty Lou, another of our friends, often helped Karen, Buck, Gale, or me, and we admired them immensely for being so bright and smart.

Miss Casey introduced us to the *Dick and Jane* reading series. Dick, Jane, Sally, and Spot became our beloved friends on paper. Their experiences were similar to our own, and fairly simple and uncomplicated. They mostly played with friends, family, and pets; rode bikes; and climbed trees. We had colorful maps and globes and textbooks that took us to faraway places and opened our minds to possibilities and opportunities that existed outside the little cocoon that we called Rockaway Beach.

There was no cafeteria provided for students at New Flint Hill

School, but all the students lived within walking distance, so we went home for a forty-five minute lunch break. Most of the mothers helped run their family businesses during the summer months but stayed home during the off-season, so they were there to greet us midday. When Francie and I popped in for lunch, Mother and our little sister, Sherry, stopped what they were doing, and we talked about the first half of our day.

When we returned from lunch during the fall and spring, we had outside recess in the schoolyard. Baseball was one of the favorite activities of the students as well as our teacher. It was not traditional baseball, however. Miss Casey devised a way that all of the students could rotate through the game in one recess and have a turn to bat. A wise woman she was to ward off the bickering that inevitably could result from a child's sense of unfairness about batting turns.

The trees in the schoolyard beckoned us to see how high we could climb. It was often challenging in our school dresses, but that was not a deterrent. Joan and Francie were the ringleaders and encouraged Karen and me to follow them in their many brave adventures. Vigorously climbing, we reached a comfortable spot and finally perched ourselves on a favorite limb. Proudly sitting atop a sturdy branch, one of them would pull a tube of lipstick from her pocket which had been snatched from our mothers' cosmetic drawers, and we all generously smeared our lips with it. With a gentle breeze blowing through our hair, we imagined that we were Hollywood movie stars enjoying the adoration of our many fans. Descending after recess and returning to the classroom, we felt empowered by our bright red cherry lips and intoxicated with the possibilities that awaited us as we looked forward to growing older and wiser.

After recess, we had silent reading time, and everyone had the opportunity to go to our library, a small separate area at the back of the one big room where we all did our work. For the most part, the students got along well, but one day, an eighth-grade boy caused quite a ruckus in the library. He became agitated about something

Miss Casey did or said, and he became more and more angry as the afternoon went on. A husky boy with a muscular build, he outmatched petite little Miss Casey, usually dressed in her black suit, silk blouse, and clunky-heeled tie shoes. But she stayed calm until the unruly student decided that he was going to take the situation into his own hands.

He started shoving her. He shoved her to the floor and held her there. Wide-eyed and stunned, my seven-year-old body froze in its chair. Eleven-year-old Francie, in contrast, hightailed it out of the building without asking for permission, sprinted across the schoolyard to our house, and informed Daddy of what was happening. Within minutes, he was at the school, had the situation under control, and was taking the boy home to his parents.

Our little school did not have detention or in-school suspension for behavioral issues, but parents took responsibility for the actions of their children. After meeting with the boy and his parents, Miss Casey and parents of the other students allowed the unruly student to return to school. He finished his eighth-grade year at New Flint Hill. The episode I observed that day in the small library of our one-room schoolhouse has remained an indelible memory, but along with the memory of a shameful act by an adolescent, I saw grace and forgiveness extended to a young man who went on to finish high school and become a productive citizen of Taney County.

Every spring, one of our school activities was to make May Day baskets from lavender, pink, and purple construction paper with matching paper handles and fill them with wildflowers gathered from the woods behind the schoolhouse. In the May Day tradition, we then scurried about the Beach hanging the colorful baskets on the doors of friends and elderly neighbors. Anonymity was a big part of this tradition, so we hung them on the door, rang the doorbell, and quickly ran away.

One year, the parents erected a May Day pole and carefully adorned it from the top center with crepe paper streamers in vibrant spring colors. With our teacher's help, we practiced the steps of the

May Day dance, and on May 1, decked out in our Sunday clothes and shiny patent leather shoes, we performed the dance for the whole community. Weaving around the May Day pole in the intricate steps we had learned strengthened our sense of dependency on each other and taught us the importance of teamwork at a very early age.

During the winter, a heavy snow did not mean a day off from school. Since we walked to school, we had to bundle up and make the trek up the hill. Girls did not wear jeans or pants to school, only dresses or skirts, and leggings and tights had not yet made the fashion scene. Mother's solution to keep our legs warm was to make us wear blue jeans under our skirts, take them off when we got to school, and put them back on before we headed home. I did not like her solution one bit, but begrudgingly, I did what she said on those cold and snowy mornings, feeling like what would be called in today's vernacular "a real dork"! Oh, how we missed our outside recess on those winter days, but we were entertained inside with games like pin the tail on the donkey, jacks, checkers, Old Maid, or Monopoly.

My first three years of school at New Flint Hill were precious. Lifelong friendships were formed, the value of education was instilled in me, and I cherished the sense of belonging that was fostered there through friendships and the support and encouragement of my teacher, Miss Casey, and my parents. The year that I turned eight, 1953, New Flint Hill School consolidated with Branson Public Schools. Big changes were on the horizon for our little band of fifteen Rockaway Beach students.

1953–1954

Sometimes years roll by, month after month, day after day, with few events standing out as significant. Children get up every day, get dressed, and go about their daily activities, including school, church, play, sports, and family time. When a year comes to an end, one often cannot name a single event that made the year different from years previous, and that can be a comforting way of life. As there is assurance and comfort in the orderliness of seasons, there is comfort in the orderliness of events in our lives. However, the school year of 1953–54 was not an ordinary one for the Michel family.

After starting school in the one-room school at age five in 1950, I stayed through my first three grades. Then the Branson School District reached out to the citizens in rural areas of Taney County seeking consolidation of its one-room schools with the Branson schools. The citizens in all of the smaller communities voted yes to send their children to Branson schools starting in September 1953, and it turned my world upside-down.

I sensed at the young age of eight that I was going into the unknown and that I would be far from the security of our little neighborhood where Mother and Daddy were just minutes away from the schoolhouse. I would have to ride the school bus eleven miles every day one way. For the first time in my life, I would be a stranger.

Of the fourteen or fifteen students in our entire school, one was my sister and one was my cousin, Karen, who was as close as one of my sisters and my lifelong playmate. I was told that there would be two full classrooms of students for each grade level in Branson. How could I ever learn all of those names and get to know that many people in my class? I was afraid of the new demands I was about to face and unwilling to believe that I would be able to survive what was being asked of me.

Mother and Daddy encouraged us all that summer before school started and tried to prepare us for a new adventure. But fear of the unknown lingered, especially for Francie and me. Francie was entering sixth grade. Sherry was entering kindergarten, so she didn't experience the same kind of fear I was feeling, but Francie probably did.

On the first day of the 1953–54 school year, there was no ringing of the school bell that had greeted the children of Rockaway since 1926. Instead, Mother and Daddy put us on a bus, which was driven by Arlie Blansit, a longtime resident of the Beach and a longtime friend of the family. He stopped in front of our Ozark giraffe rock bungalow early on Tuesday morning, the day after Labor Day, and we three girls, dressed in carefully chosen new school clothes, stepped gingerly onto the bus with mixed emotions. Fear, anxiety, butterflies in the tummy, and a little bit of excitement overwhelmed us as the bus plodded past the old familiar schoolhouse where we normally would have been gathering for the first day and headed toward the steep hill that would take us away from the Beach and west toward Branson.

Karen and I sat together toward the front of the bus, silently supporting each other for eleven long miles of winding hills and curves, united in this situation over which we had no control. We strengthened and encouraged each other just by being together in the adventure, and we hung onto the hope that we would not be separated by the two classrooms of fourth-graders. We assured each other that if we could just be in the same room, we could survive.

However, upon arrival at Branson Elementary on Pacific Street that first Tuesday after Labor Day—a warm, sunny day with a hint of autumn in the air—I learned that Karen would be in Mrs. Awberry's room and I would be in Miss Brown's room. I had never felt so alone, so abandoned, so afraid. I knew no one in the room, and I was heartbroken. Karen and I would not be together during the day for the first time since we were five years old. I kept asking myself how I could be treated so cruelly! How could they be so insensitive as to separate us?

During that first Tuesday morning of school in a place that was both new and frightening, I did make some friends. Mike Eiserman, Jenny Caudill, David Magness, and others made me feel welcome to Branson Elementary. Miss Brown, our pretty, dark-haired teacher, was slender, immaculately groomed and dressed, kind, soft-spoken, and interested in each of us. She showed it by her attentiveness to every detail of our first day of school.

It was actually Miss Reba Mae Brown who inspired me from that very day to dream about becoming a teacher myself. She loved children, and her gentle manner in the classroom throughout that year displayed a teaching style that encouraged me and inspired me to achieve. Mrs. Awberry, the other fourth-grade teacher, had a personality quite the opposite of Miss Brown's. She was loud and bold, quite a jokester, and I was totally afraid of her. She was a good teacher, highly regarded by parents, and her students loved her, but her style of teaching made me uncomfortable.

My cousin Judy tells the story of how she and another classmate wouldn't stop talking during class one day, so Mrs. Awberry put them in the closet for a while to think about their unacceptable behavior. I'm thankful to this day that Miss Brown was my teacher.

It was an adjustment to have only one grade level in a classroom, but I adapted easily and soon learned that it offered many advantages. I loved having new friends and found it quite easy to remember all of their names in contrast to what I had feared. We had sports teams, a cafeteria with good home-cooked meals, spelling and math bees with stiff competition, and field trips. It didn't take long to realize that the advantages of a big school far outweighed the disadvantages, and I fell in love with the Branson School District.

A great love for the Branson Pirates has stayed with me all of my life, only slightly diminished by my loyalty to Forsyth R3 Schools, ten miles to the east of Branson, when I took a teaching job there in 1998. While I was teaching in the Forsyth School District, if a match between the two teams took place, I had to root for my Forsyth students.

During the 1953–54 school year, another noteworthy event took place in our little town of Branson. Late one afternoon, when we had all of the cottages rented, Mother and Daddy took Francie, Sherry, and me for a ride out west of Branson on the winding country road called Highway 76. There was only one small white-framed building on the road: a field office for the State Forestry Department. The road was a narrow two-lane, and some of it was not blacktopped. We drove six to eight miles west of downtown Branson and stopped up on a high mountain in Shepherd of the Hills country. We got out of the car and gazed at the valley below us.

Mother said, "Girls, take a good look down in that valley, because in the near future, it will be completely covered with a new lake. It will never look the same."

What they were sharing with us was the news that the US Army Corps of Engineers had announced plans to build what was going to be called Table Rock Dam to prevent flooding from the raging torrents of the White River. The flooding along Lake Taneycomo because of the White River caused devastation to property and residents in Forsyth, Rockaway Beach, and Branson in the first half of the twentieth century.

Flood prevention was eagerly anticipated by people along the shores of Lake Taneycomo. Little did we know that it would change the course of history for our town and our area because of the magnificent lake that would soon be created with the building of the dam. This gigantic feat in the rocky hills and dales of Ozark Mountain Country was taken on by the Morrison-Knudson

Construction Company, with headquarters in Boise, Idaho. Branson was on the cusp of dramatic growth because of the dam and the lake it created.

Of greater impact, however, than the changes to our community was the impact this announcement would eventually have on my life and the course of events it would create for me in future years. It was life-changing and huge!

As I finally settled into my first year in Branson schools, I began to realize that many activities and opportunities were available to me that I did not have in the one-room school. I was a big fan of boys' basketball, and along with my cousins Karen and Judy became a fourth-grade cheerleader for a group of five boys who had been playing basketball together since first or second grade. They were a special group, because they continued to play as a cohesive team through our senior year, when we played in the state championship game in Columbia and lost the final game by one point. What an experience to be part of that journey with my classmates all of those years.

Mother and Daddy both enjoyed watching the Branson Pirates high school basketball team, and they took us to basketball games all over southwest Missouri. Many a night during basketball season, we would hurry in from school, have a quick supper, and head out to places twenty to seventy miles away to support our team. During the winter months, it was not uncommon for a surprise snowstorm to drift in while we were cheering for the Pirates, and then Daddy would have to drive these Ozark hills and curves with a sheet of ice and sleet.

I have memories of him proclaiming, more than once, "We are not going to another game if there is even a hint of snow!" Forecasts then were not as precise as they are now, and while I felt sorry for him having to drive us home in that treacherous weather, I was secretly pretty excited that we were getting snow and probably wouldn't have to go to school the next day.

Along about September of that year, we girls got some amazing news from Mother and Daddy. We had heard stories from both of them about how they wanted a boy, but instead, after Francie, they had two more baby girls. When Francie was twelve, I was nine, and Sherry was seven, we learned that we were going to have a new baby in April. We were confident that our new baby would be a boy, but we had to wait until that time to see.

We talked about this new addition to our family, and Francie, being twelve, knew she was quite capable of being the responsible big sister. At nine, I wasn't so sure about all that entailed, and seven-year-old Sherry just knew that he, hopefully, or she would be a new little person to add to her doll domain. All through the school year, we anticipated the arrival of our new sibling. We were enchanted with the idea.

Mother and Daddy were thrilled as well, but they began thinking in more practical terms and realized that our 1940s-era stone bungalow was already bursting at the seams with three rambunctious girls. Our bedroom—an enclosed porch where we three girls shared a full-size bed—actually served as the office for our business during the summer months. Beside the bed was Daddy's old maple desk and the small matching chair with its vinyl green cover where our guests registered for their stay at the resort.

We girls didn't necessarily perceive the arrangement as unusual, but we were sometimes annoyed when early-bird guests rang the doorbell at 7 a.m. to check out and awakened us from a deep summer sleep. Occasionally some uppity guest would proclaim, "I thought this was the office. It looks like a bedroom!"

With the resort growing now to about twelve cottages housing fifty to sixty guests nightly, our parents felt that the time had come to build a new home. In September of 1953, Daddy and his crew of brothers began working on the new house. The exterior of the home was native white creek rock that Daddy made trip after trip south into Arkansas to gather from public creek beds, where it was available for the taking. He and Uncle Lee did most of the construction on the house throughout the fall and winter months, and in March 1954, we moved seventy-five feet east from our little bungalow to the new house. It was an exciting event!

Our ranch-style home was 82 feet long and 2,600 square feet on one level. By today's McMansion standards, it doesn't sound extraordinary, but with its three large bedrooms, two bathrooms (a rarity in Taney County at that time), and a kitchen large enough to accommodate our yellow rectangular Formica table that could seat ten people, it was exceptionally nice. It featured modern appliances, including a dishwasher which Daddy rarely allowed us to use because he thought it would prohibitively increase our electricity and water bills. Since dishwashing and cleaning up in the kitchen was a regular chore for Francie, Sherry, and me, we often wondered in later years why he installed it in the first place! Once in a great while, if we had a large crowd gather for a holiday, he or Mother would reluctantly say, "Go ahead and use the dishwasher today, girls." On the rare occasions when that did happen, we thought we had chalked up a major coup.

We had an extremely large laundry room and shelf-lined pantry and storage room. In the front of the house, we had a large connecting dining and living room and a clearly defined office constructed with knotty pine walls. When guests entered our new office, they knew they were in a place of business—friendly, but professional. No more opportunity for uppity guests to think they were entering a bedroom in a hillbilly home.

During the days leading up to the big day, Mother had a perception of how she wanted the move to take place, and she carried it out with the skill and finesse of a master drill sergeant. New furniture appropriate for each room was delivered first. In the large bedroom we shared, Francie, Sherry, and I had two double beds, a large dresser, a chest of drawers, and a desk. Daddy built separate closets for each of us with shelves lining the walls and racks placed at eye level for us individually. As we grew through the years, the racks were raised to stay at eye level and fit our hanging clothes.

New dining room furniture was delivered, and then a new

sofa, chairs, and tables for the living room. Once the furniture was arranged, we carried box after box of our personal belongings to the new house. Mother worked night and day while eight months pregnant during those early March days to set up the kitchen with every teacup, bowl, pot, and pan in its perfect place. On the last night before we slept in our new home, she ironed pink and blue checkered bedspreads and curtains for our bedroom to match the blue fixtures in our bathroom, and placed what we would now call freshly starched vintage doilies and lamps on our dresser and chest of drawers. Her efforts, so obviously a labor of love, created a lovely memory for the first night in our new home.

A few weeks before the birth of our new sibling, Mother had a weekly appointment with her doctor in Springfield. During the early fifties, most people who left their homes, especially to go to Springfield for an appointment, dressed in what we would call today their Sunday clothes. Mother and Daddy were no exception. For this late March appointment on a cold and windy day, Mother wore her dark brown matching two-piece maternity skirted suit with a touch of cream-colored piping on the lapel, her brown snakeskin pumps, and a pretty green wool heavy winter coat. Daddy wore a double-breasted suit, overcoat, and felt-brim hat with a slight upturn in the back.

As they left for their late-afternoon appointment, they dropped us off to spend the night with Aunt Virginia and Uncle Lee, who lived just one block up the hill from us, because they anticipated getting home well after dark. We loved staying with our aunt and uncle, whom we considered almost second parents. When we went to bed that night, we were prepared to get on the bus with Karen the next morning and begin our day with little interruption to our normal schedule. What a surprise we had that morning when we awakened to an unexpected ice and snow storm!

As we looked out Aunt Virginia's big picture window toward the street, we gasped and screamed in delight at the scene of ice-covered limbs and glistening icicles hanging from the rooftop, and we knew we would not be going to school. And then, much to our disbelief on that early snowy morning, we saw a sight on the hill heading down to our house that amazed and confused us. Mother and Daddy, still dressed in the clothes they had on when they left for their appointment the day before, were carefully trying to navigate the slick and hilly terrain. Mother, eight months pregnant, still had on her snakeskin high heels and appeared to be walking on eggshells; Daddy, still in his overcoat and hat, was holding on to her for dear life. We couldn't imagine why we were seeing this sight—it didn't make sense!

Confronted with the same surprise storm on their way home, Daddy had crept along the winding, hilly roads of old Highway 65. He managed to keep control under stressful circumstances for nearly forty miles, but on the very last leg of the trip, only two miles from home on a county road never visited by snow maintenance trucks, he lost control on a slippery spot, and their boatlike four-door '54 Olds veered ever so gently off the road and got stuck. Trees surrounded them, but as if guided by the hand of God, they were spared a collision that could have been heartbreaking.

After catching their breath and realizing they were okay, they assessed the situation and decided to stay put. With a stash of supplies including warm blankets placed in the trunk of the car for just such an emergency, they decided to hunker down through the long dark hours of the icy March night. As morning began to dawn and the sun slowly crept out of the stormy sky of the night before, they began to traverse the last two icy miles. Their trek over the ice-covered roads took two hours, but they finally reached the warmth and comfort of their beautiful new home in the hills.

They didn't stop to pick us up when they passed Uncle Lee's house, but stunned while gazing at the scene before our very eyes, full of concern and unanswered questions, we grabbed our coats, and Uncle Lee walked us down the hill to join them. After Daddy made Mother comfortable in her warm robe and fuzzy house shoes with a cup of hot tea, he lit a fire in the fireplace. He and all of his girls were safe at home together, and tales of the long night began to unfold.

Less than a month after the icy road escapade, our little brother Edwin Vernon was born pink and healthy at St. John's Hospital in Springfield. At long last, Daddy and Mother got their boy, and we girls had a new baby brother we adored. We were allowed to miss school on the day we brought him home from the hospital, and we couldn't take our eyes off him.

On this particular bright sunny day, Ed was snuggled securely in Mother's arms in the front seat. Francie, Sherry, and I were thankful for him and the good feeling that we didn't have to worry about icy roads as we journeyed back to Rockaway Beach. We helped Mother bathe him. We learned about the fairly complex process of sterilizing his Pyrex glass bottles by boiling them, and we learned how to feed him. As the weeks went by, we became more comfortable holding him without assistance and playing with him like one of our dolls.

One evening, all three of us were playing with six-week-old Edwin up on our bed, and our worst nightmare occurred: he fell off the bed onto the solid hardwood floor. We screamed and cried. Rushing into our bedroom, Daddy picked the baby up and remained calm, but Mother was inconsolable. I had never seen her as I saw her during the first few minutes after the accident happened. She screamed, ran in circles, and threw herself on the floor sobbing.

Daddy, remaining calm, called our doctor, who advised us to try to keep the baby awake for as long as we could. We rubbed his forehead and cheeks with a cold, wet cloth. He stayed awake for a few hours, and then he slept. Thankfully, he suffered no permanent injury.

The nine-month school year of 1953–54 was a roller coaster of adventures and emotion for the Michel family: new school, new house, a new baby brother, and some wild rides up and down the curvy tracks of life that we weren't expecting. What I didn't know then, at that end of my fourth-grade school year, was that at the age of nine, I had met my future husband.

Choose Your Friends Carefully

When I became a sixth-grade teacher, the first day of school was spent getting acquainted with my students, and I was the first person to start making introductions. I began by telling my students that I was born in Taney County and grew up in Rockaway Beach. I then spoke on the virtues of choosing your friends wisely even at a young age, and I proceeded to share with the young children, whose first-day-of-school eager eyes and ears absorbed every word spoken by their new teacher, that I had met my husband when I was younger than they were at the beginning of their sixth-grade year.

After a few snickers because they found it hard to believe that a teacher actually had a life so personal as to have had a boyfriend, I explained that we were schoolmates when I was in fourth grade and he was in fifth grade. I shared with them that I thought he was pretty cute in the fifth grade, and their snickers turned into outright giggles and wide-eyed listening. It was a story that humanized their teacher and made them realize that friendships at an early age could have a significant impact upon future events in their lives.

In 1941, the US Army Corps of Engineers received funding from Congress through the Flood Control Act to build Table Rock Dam west of Branson as a way to control flooding and provide hydroelectric power to communities in southern Missouri and northern Arkansas. With its 850 miles of shoreline, Table Rock Lake was expected to become a popular recreational lake as well. Construction, however, was delayed in 1941 by US involvement in World War II, and then again in the early 1950s with our involvement in the Korean War.

Finally, in October of 1954, construction on the dam began, with hundreds of people employed by the Corps of Engineers and Morrison-Knudsen Construction Company moving into the Branson area. A huge influx of new students—who came to be known affectionately as the "dam kids"—brought new life to the small Branson school district. The dam kids brought with them from their many moves all over the country a touch of worldliness we had not experienced in our sleepy little town.

Branson had a reputation for being partly rural and partly a cute little fishing town known for Jim Owen's float trips up and down the White River. It hosted only a fraction of the tourists who flocked to Rockaway Beach, but this was about to change with the convergence of people who came here to work on the dam and eventually the tourists who would enjoy the magnificent lake about to be created. Many of the Morrison-Knudsen families knew each other because they moved from location to location together when dams were being built across America and the world. Two of these families were the Harold Maxwell family and the Carl Whetstone family.

Harold was the general superintendent of construction on the dam, and Carl was the chief electrical superintendent. The families were not related, but Pam Maxwell and David Whetstone as infants shared quilt pallets on the floor as their mothers doted over them, and they were lifelong best friends when they entered fifth grade in September 1954 at the old elementary school sitting on top of the hill at the corner of Pacific and Sixth Streets.

Pam and I connected almost immediately in the fall of 1954. I admired her long blond hair, pixie freckled face, and bubbly personality, and I loved being her friend. The dam kids were outgoing; few were shy or inhibited the way children sometimes are when they enter a new school. They jumped right into school, community, and church activities, playing in the band and sports and participating in Boy Scouts.

As my friendship with Pam blossomed, she kept talking about her friend David. When we moved into our new octagonal-shaped school building on Sixth Street, one block south of the old elementary building, right before Thanksgiving of 1954, I finally met David Whetstone. My fourth-grade wing with Miss Brown and David's fifth-grade wing with Mrs. Yandell were in close proximity, and I kept watching him as he confidently talked to his friends and classmates. My apprehension about entering a new school that fall was still fresh in my mind, but David behaved as if he had never attended school anywhere else. I was attracted to that kind of confidence and urbanity, and I began wondering if he might talk to me.

Eventually, he spoke to me, and I spoke back, and we became friends. When he asked for one of my school pictures that fall, we exchanged, and I still have his 1954–55 photo. During the years that the dam kids stayed in Branson—through the 1958 school year—David and I went to Saturday afternoon movies together at the old Owen's Theater on Commercial Street. We sat together at ballgames and swam in the frigid waters of the Sammy Lane Resort swimming pool with our friends.

Red Ormsbee, our beloved longtime band director, took us on band trips all school year as he entered us in every contest and parade in southwest Missouri. David played trombone, I played flute, and we spent many Saturdays traveling the winding narrow roads of the area going to regional parades, competitions, and musical events. Our band uniforms—tailored, military-like, and characteristic of the 1950s—required a stiffly starched white shirt and a man's tie knotted with military precision. Never having learned how to make the knot in my tie, I relied on Daddy to tie it for me every time I left the house for a band trip.

During my seventh-grade year, as I complained about the discomfort of wearing a tie all day long, David told me that he knew how to tie a knot in a man's tie and offered to do it for me the next time we had to wear our band uniforms. I learned quickly that for him to tie the knot correctly, he had to put his arms around me from the back to tie it to perfection, and I decided that was a fine arrangement. After that, when Daddy asked me as I was leaving the house for a band trip if I wanted him to fix my tie, I replied, "No, David Whetstone will do it!"

At the end of my seventh-grade year, the massive Table Rock Dam project was completed. Table Rock Lake was rapidly becoming a popular tourist destination with its vastly deep, calm, and warm water. As this project came to its conclusion, our wonderful, new dam friends who had moved into the community began to move on to the next project. Harold Maxwell became ill during the final stages of the dam's completion and lost his life to cancer, so Pam and her mother stayed in Branson. The Whetstone family, however, moved to Gadsden, Alabama, where Carl began work on another dam.

When David left that summer at the end of his eighth-grade year and my seventh, we said our goodbyes, and life went on for both of us. I finished junior high and entered high school engaged in many activities, including sports, music, and drama. I loved being a Branson Pirate. Once in a while, David and I would write to each other, and he told me all about his high school activities in Gadsden. He played football and participated in band activities—and, of course, began noticing girls.

He often wrote about one young lady, JoAnn, who obviously had captured his attention and admiration. Since he was in a world completely separate from mine, I was glad that he was enjoying his new school and making nice friends. In his letters, he told stories about his friends and some of the fun things they did. Gadsden High School was much larger than Branson High School, and with his band and football activities, he got to do things I could only dream about. In my occasional letter to him, I talked about my school activities and things going on with my family in Rockaway.

About two years after the Whetstone family moved to Alabama,

David made a trip back to Branson to visit Pam and her mother. One cold winter Saturday evening around seven thirty, our doorbell rang. Mother answered it, and then she came into the living room where our family was watching one of our favorite television shows, *Your Hit Parade*, and said, "Marilyn, David is here to see you."

My response was, "David who?"

She couldn't remember his last name, and we had a rapid but brief series of questions and answers trying to establish who was at the front door to see me. When I discovered that it was David Whetstone, I was surprised. He had made the eleven-mile trip east from Branson to Rockaway, according to his account, "to say hello." We stayed there with the family and tried to get caught up with each other about our high school lives in separate states.

One of the first things he showed me that night was a side-profile photo of a beautiful young lady with golden ringlets halfway down her back. When I asked him who she was, he replied, "JoAnn." He told me about JoAnn, her family, and their friendship. He also told me about his friend Benny and his part-time job working for the beauty supply company owned by Benny's parents. Mother and Daddy, Francie, and Sherry joined in the conversation as David sat and visited with me. It was easy and comfortable to have him in our home.

I hadn't seen him for more than two years, but as he left the house that cold winter evening, I secretly confided to Mother at the tender age of fourteen that I was going to marry David Whetstone someday. She laughed and ignored me, but I felt it strongly in my young heart. I don't think he had any inkling of such a radical idea. He was enamored with JoAnn! I, on the other hand, was undeterred.

The surprise visit was pleasant, and David asked me to sit with him at the upcoming Pirates basketball game. I agreed and told him I would see him there. When he and Pam walked into the gym, they found me waiting for them in the bleachers. We had a fun evening, and then he left Branson to go back to Gadsden. We continued to exchange occasional letters for another couple of years (this was well before the day of texts, email, or cell phones). I shared stories about my high school friends and relationships, and he did the same.

During my junior year in high school, our family made a trip through the south visiting Aunt Libby (Mother's youngest sister) and her husband, Uncle Bert, in Pensacola, Florida. When I learned from Daddy that we would be traveling back through Biloxi, Mississippi, I realized that we would be somewhat close to Alabama and asked if we could go through Gadsden to see David. Being the adventurous and impulsive traveler that he was, Daddy was only too happy to divert from the planned route and see some new country. He told that me if I worked it out with my Gadsden friend, we would go see him.

During the years they lived in Branson, I had not met David's parents, so it struck me as a good time to do so. When we were settled into our motel room in Biloxi, I went to the office to make the phone call; at that time, private phones were not available in individual rooms. With butterflies in my tummy, I slowly dialed the number on the coin-operated public phone. When Mrs. Reecie Whetstone answered the phone, I carefully plunked the exact number of quarters and dimes into their slots, identified who I was, and asked to speak to David. I hoped he was home, because this was my only chance to connect with him; upon leaving Biloxi early the next day, Daddy would have to make a decision which way to turn as we traveled north from the Gulf Coast: north and east toward Gadsden, or north and west toward Rockaway Beach?

As it turned out, David *was* home. At first, he sounded surprised to hear from me. A senior in high school, he was cordial but aloof. Suddenly jarred by my boldness at making the phone call, I became slightly embarrassed at my own presumption that he would be interested in talking to me. After a few minutes of casual conversation, and always mindful of the need to feed the pay phone if my minutes expired, I got right to the point, telling David that I would like to drive with my family to Gadsden to visit him.

There was what I perceived to be an uncomfortable silence on his end, and then he said, "Marilyn, I have a girlfriend, but do come on."

That was all I needed to hear. I told him it was nice to visit with him, hung up, went straight to our room, and said, "Daddy, there is no need to go to Gadsden." The next morning, bright and early, we headed north and west.

As my junior year rolled into my senior year, our letters became fewer and farther between. My thoughts of him dwindled as I began to think more of my future. I enjoyed my senior year in high school and looked forward to a new chapter in my life as I prepared for college in the fall.

In April of the following year, as I looked forward to the Buccaneer Ball, our high school spring formal dance, and all of the other senior year activities, I received an unexpected phone call. It was a person-to-person call for Marilyn Michel coming from Wichita Falls, Texas. Mother answered the phone, but she had no idea who was calling me person-to-person from a place about which we knew nothing. I took the call, and it was David calling from Sheppard Air Force Base, where he was taking ICBM (intercontinental ballistic missile) technical training. I had not spoken to him since I had called him from Biloxi.

As history repeats itself, he seemed a bit uncomfortable with the conversation, and I sensed that I was in control of it more than he was. Somewhat awkwardly, he explained what was going on in his life and asked about mine. Then he said why he was calling. He and a buddy had a few days of furlough from their training, and he asked if he could travel to Rockaway to see me.

I had a boyfriend with whom I had been going to movies, ball games, and dances at the pavilion. So I replied, "I have a boyfriend, but do come anyway!"

He came to Rockaway during late spring of 1962, and though I had no idea at the time, his visit was a life-changing event for both of us. I was young, only seventeen, but I felt like I was reuniting with my soulmate and my best friend. Because I had started first grade when I was barely five years old, I graduated high school at sixteen. College was on the horizon for me, but I liked David Whetstone very much. Did we have a chance to develop a lasting friendship when our worlds were so very far apart? He was awaiting orders for transfer to who knows where, and I was beginning my freshman year at Southwest Missouri State.

We were young, but young love is sweet. I admired him. We shared the same Christian beliefs. He was ambitious and believed in himself. I was love-struck, once again, with the little fifth-grade boy I met when I was in fourth grade. The little fifth-grade boy had grown into a handsome black-haired young man who, I thought, looked like Eddie Fisher, the popular 1950s singer and movie star.

I Am My Brother's Keeper

Shortly after we moved into the big house in 1954, Daddy and Mother decided that modern resort guests expected a private swimming pool with their accommodations. Lake Taneycomo was popular for swimming and boating, but a large public pool had been built on the Beach, and visionary that he was, Daddy believed it would be a wise business move to have a private pool on our property. He and his brothers set out to build it during the fall and winter of 1954.

To crack through the rock, they had to use dynamite and heavy excavation equipment, and they carefully chose the weather-perfect days throughout the cold months of winter to pour concrete. By spring of 1955, just in time for the seniors to start arriving in April, we had a handsome pool, including a separate "kiddie's pool," as it was advertised on our brochures. Both were filled with sparkling clean, clear water. The concrete decks were outfitted with colorful umbrellas, tables, and chairs, and decorated with pots of geraniums, chrysanthemums, impatiens, and petunias.

It was unbelievable how the corner beside our rambling ranch-style house could be transformed so quickly from a homespun rock flower garden into a beautiful forty-by-sixty-foot entertainment area for our guests, with a pinball games and arcade area and an elevated patio and deck built around a massive walnut tree to add interest and aesthetics. Daddy's God-given ability to imagine and then create with his own two hands was a blessing in our business. And with the help and added talents of his brothers, the blessings multiplied, as they say, exponentially.

Sunday afternoons were set aside for family visits, even during the busy summer months. Uncle (as we called Daddy's twin) and his wife, Nora, whom we called Auntie, often came to visit, bringing cousins Ronnie, Sharon, and Janeyce as well as Auntie's identical twin, Orie. Uncle Charlie and Aunt Jewell often popped in with their girls, Liz and Judy. Sometimes both families came at the same time, and an impromptu party began.

Most family visits were unannounced; calling ahead was not expected, and such get-togethers were always welcomed and enjoyed by parents and children. As much as possible, during the summer months on Sunday afternoons, whatever Mother and Daddy were doing stopped and the "company"—as we called aunts, uncles, cousins, or any other visitors—became the focus for as long as they wanted to stay. The cousins often swam in the pool while the parents sat in the big comfortable living room of our home sipping sweet iced tea, so that Mother and Daddy could be close to the office in case the guests needed anything.

About the same time the pool was added, we got a large black-and-white console TV—one of the last families on the Beach to do so. Francie, Sherry, and I felt like everybody in the world had a television except us. The Puchtas, our parents' best friends, parents of Joan and owners of Kenny's Court just down the hill a half block from us, had one. Aunt Virginia, Uncle Lee, and Karen had one. We had a console radio with a record player in our living room to provide our nightly entertainment, but it wasn't the same. I used to glare at the console radio, imagining what it would be like to have in its place the magic of a picture along with words in our living room.

Once we finally got our TV, the cousins would end the afternoon finding something to watch on TV before they had to go home. *The Little Rascals* and all of their antics was one of our favorites.

The six Michel brothers had a tight close bond—all of them, all through their lives—and they never went too many days without seeing or talking to each other. They all lived within a fifteen-mile radius of Rockaway and Branson, and each held the deep conviction that "I am my brother's keeper." Sunday afternoons were family visiting time and a time to check in just to learn how the week had gone. Great philosophical issues were not discussed, politics was not of any interest, and gossip was not welcome. Conversation revolved around the brothers' work. Three were business owners in the communities of Rockaway and Branson, and three were farmers who also worked in Uncle Ernie's construction business. The wives discussed putting up peaches or okra or green beans; who among the relatives or friends had been ill; who was getting married; and who had died.

During visits, the brothers learned from each other about the needs of their sisters or widowed cousins and discussed ways to help them. Ruby Persinger, their beloved first cousin and a recent widow with three school-age boys, was looked after by the brothers, and they offered a helping hand when needed. Three of their sisters—Lilly, Della, and Pearl—lived within the same fifteen-mile area, and they, too, were looked after by their brothers.

Aunt Lilly lived in Rockaway with her family, and Daddy was never out of touch with her. One year when the Buccaneer Ball rolled around, he loaned her son our brand-new 1954 two-toned blue and white Oldsmobile. Cousin Gordon was handsome with his dark brown eyes, wavy black hair, and white sport coat as he traveled in style to pick up his pretty blonde date decked out in her pastel-colored formal with crinoline petticoats. Gordon did not come asking to borrow Daddy's car; quite the opposite. Daddy offered it because he wanted Gordon to have a special evening. Love, loyalty, and a strong family bond were his motivators.

On their way to the Buccaneer Ball, Gordon and his date stopped by the house to say hello to Uncle Vernie and Aunt Louise and take pictures. I was one impressed little girl that evening with these handsome high schoolers embarking upon an evening to make beautiful memories in a gym decked out in crepe paper streamers and flashing lanterns hung from the ceiling.

Aunt Della was a single mom raising her three boys alone, so the brothers felt a responsibility to look after her. Divorced, she had her own home, and the brothers made sure she had wood for the winter and were always willing to help with house repairs, yard work, or transportation. Uncle, who lived a short distance from her, made sure she got to doctors' appointments and especially church. She raised her three sons without a driver's license. She never owned a car, but she had six faithful and loving brothers.

Next to the last of the twelve Michel siblings was Aunt Pearl, who was born with the neurological condition known as epilepsy. She was prone to sudden seizures that she called spells and wore braces on her legs for most of her life. She attended high school, but in the early part of the twentieth century little treatment or medication was available for her condition, or at least accessible to the large family, and she suffered the consequences throughout her life.

Although Pearl was unable to care for herself, her family was unwilling to institutionalize her. Grandpa Michel, widowed when Pearl was still a teenager, took care of her for many years. When he was no longer able to do so, the six brothers and their families decided to take her into their homes on a rotating basis. Each family would include her in their lives for several months at a time, and then she would move on to the next family. Aunt Pearl loved her brood of nieces and nephews, and we loved her. Even when she was an adult, we thought of her more as one our own age. She was very forthright, to the point of being blunt about everything, and we knew we would learn the truth about a situation from her when others may have been more rose-colored.

Pearl lived with her brothers for many years with this rotating arrangement until Uncle Exie fixed up a little cottage on the homestead where she could live independently only a few hundred yards from the home where she was born, under the watchful eye of Uncle Exie and Aunt Rose. During the last years of her life, she was in a nursing home in Branson and enjoyed meeting people who became her friends. When we visited her there during the last years of her life, she appeared to be happy and content with her circumstances.

Cousin Judy, Uncle Charlie's daughter, tells about the building of their large stone home in the early 1950s about four miles north of Branson. The family was living in a small house in the rolling hills of their countryside property when Uncle Charlie and Aunt Jewell decided to take on the building of a new home. After working all week in Uncle's construction business, Uncle Charlie worked after hours and on weekends to build their new home, which included a large spacious kitchen and dining room, a living room with a native stone fireplace, and a screened-in porch facing west to capture glorious Ozark sunsets. Of their four children, only Liz and Judy were still living at home, so the house plans called for two large bedrooms and a hall bathroom, very typical of 1950s ranch-style architecture.

Drawing on their natural craftsmanship abilities, Uncle Charlie's five brothers voluntarily joined him on Saturdays to help with the construction of his family's new home. He related to his children later in life how important it was to him in the years that followed to go unsolicited to their homes or businesses to help them with projects when he could.

The devotion the brothers had to each other was shared by the devotion among the six wives. They loved each other, enjoyed being with each other, laughed often, and cooked and shared wonderful meals. As Mother often commented, "It is unusual that there is no fussing among the in-laws, but it's a blessing."

In reflecting back on these stories, I am convinced that some people will not believe them because they sound so Pollyannaish, or I will be accused of telling a truth tempered by time and age. I stand firm on the accuracy of my memories, partly because they are so deeply ingrained in my heart, but also because when sprinklings of the cousins get together, we share and affirm the same stories and have similar memories, with few differences in the recollection of events.

I never heard Mother or Daddy say, "You always need to take care of family." I did, however, see that belief lived out by my parents and my uncles and aunts. I never saw a begrudging attitude or heard any complaining from aunts, uncles, or cousins about the time, effort, and sacrifice made to take care of extended family. When a family member was sick, the whole clan rallied around that individual.

My own daddy was the first of the six brothers to pass from this life at the age of fifty-seven from cancer. During one of the last nights he was alive, his five brothers and their wives surrounded him in the hospital to share his journey through the valley of the shadow of death. As they left the room on the last night, the brothers and their wives were all together. Sherry stood at the door watching them and tells the sweet story of each of the five brothers walking down the long hospital corridor in an unplanned procession holding the hand of his beloved wife while Mother stayed in the room grieving and holding the hand of her beloved husband, whose remaining hours on this earth were numbered.

Genesis 4:8–9 from the Bible (NIV) reads:

And while they were in the field, Cain attacked his brother Abel and killed him. Then the Lord said to Cain, "Where is your brother Abel?"

"I do not know," he replied. "Am I my brother's keeper?"

The Michel brothers never asked that question. Quite the opposite, their actions and their lives exemplified their deep belief and firm conviction that "I am my brother's keeper."

Romans 8:28

When Kenny asked anyone celebrating a birthday during the week to come forward, the birthday girl or boy, teenager or adult, stepped briskly to the front of the room. A five-year-old held five pennies or a nickel, while a thirty-year-old had a quarter and a nickel. Little ones often had their coins secured tightly in a handkerchief, while old folks had a dollar bill or a couple of the larger-sized coins in hand to clunk into the handcrafted and perfectly painted miniature white church with steeple, about the size of the birdhouse that sat permanently on Kenny's podium. The congregation then proceeded in unison to recite the poem by Louise Gunderson Shimon that we knew by heart:

> Many happy returns on the day of thy birth
>
> Many seasons of sunshine be given
>
> May our Father in heaven prepare thee on earth
>
> For a beautiful birthday in heaven.

This beloved custom was part of our fifteen- to twenty-minute gathering as a whole group, where Mother and Daddy sat as bookends on the sturdy brown wooden folding chairs with Francie, Sherry, and I between them, and Ed on Mother's lap. Kenny greeted us and gave a brief overview of the Sunday school lesson, which was the same topic in our quarterlies, children and adults alike. We sang a few hymns and stood facing the American and Christian flags to say the Pledge of Allegiance and the Christian Pledge of Allegiance.

The leader of our Sunday school, Kenny Puchta, whom we called our superintendent, was not trained in seminary, but with his opening remarks and eloquent prayers, he most assuredly was our Christian leader. He spoke from his heart. God anointed him to serve a small group of faithful believers.

I had started taking piano lessons at age five, and it was natural to play hymns as I got a little older. By the time I was ten, during the summers when Hazel, our regular pianist, could not attend because of her business responsibilities, I began playing during our singing time. I learned "Jesus Loves Me," "Standing on the Promises," and "What a Friend We Have in Jesus," among many other old-time favorites. One of our standards as the Sunday school hour ended was "God Be With You Till We Meet Again."

I played often during my growing-up years, and in his gracious manner, Kenny would ask, "Marilyn, what are we going to sing today?" What I chose and had practiced, we played. If I stumbled through some of the songs, I was still praised by Kenny with love and appreciation for doing such a nice job. Unconditional love exemplified!

On Saturday night, Francie, Sherry, and I had to study for our Sunday school lesson. After we took baths and put on our pajamas, we sat on the floor in front of the fireplace. Under the supervision of Mother or Daddy, we read the lesson, answered the questions in our quarterly, and colored the pictures that illustrated the lesson for the next day.

Perfect attendance for a calendar year was our goal, after which time we would get a dangling attachment to the Perfect Attendance button that was earned the first year we attended fifty-two Sundays without missing even one. Our attachments for up to eight years to the original button hung two to three inches below it, and we wore them proudly to Sunday school. Even when we traveled, Mother and

Daddy made it a priority to visit a Sunday school wherever we found ourselves on the Sabbath.

During those many Sundays, we were introduced to Bible characters, and their stories came alive to us through the faithfulness of our mothers, who were willing to prepare the lessons. I heard the story about Moses and how he was placed in a basket and hidden in the water at about the time Edwin was a new baby, and I was horrified at the idea of putting him in a basket and placing it on the waters of Lake Taneycomo to float to who knows where. Mother and Daddy had to quell my fears and reassure me that baby brother Edwin would not experience the same fate as baby Moses.

The moms rotated through the years to different age groups, and they recruited some of us in our teen years to help in the children's classes. We accepted the responsibility of teaching the younger children and found ourselves in need of deeper Bible study so that we would be prepared. Taking on the responsibility as a teenager of teaching a class put us in the position of being a role model in the community, and I tried to take it seriously.

The opportunity to work with children as a Sunday school teacher contributed to my desire to become a teacher later in life. Romans 8:28 says, "And we know that in all things God works for the good of those who love him, who have been called according to his purpose" (NIV). Could it be that He begins preparing us even as children to do the life work He has planned for us?

Kenny arrived at the church fifteen minutes before Sunday school to ring the heavy cast-iron bell that was a holdover from New Flint Hill School. Its loud peals rang through the Beach area to let folks know it was time to get on up to the church. Sunday school time was nine to ten, and most of us then left immediately to go to church services in Branson. Our family went to First Presbyterian on Main Street. After church, we headed home, always anticipating the homemade meal Mother had waiting.

She spent most of Saturday afternoon preparing a special salad or dessert for Sunday dinner, and on Sunday morning, she arose early and put a roast in the oven or made fried chicken or some other favorite main dish that was ready to eat as soon as we walked through the door from church. Ravishingly hungry by noon after the morning activities, we looked forward to being greeted by the aroma of something really good cooking in the oven. It was not unheard of for mother to don an apron while still in her high heels and hat to add the final touches to the Sunday dinner we so eagerly anticipated.

On March 23, 1958, four years after Edwin's birth, another little brother, Michael Reese, was born. Sadly, he was stillborn, and we never got to hold him or see him. During the long ordeal for my parents at St. John's Hospital in Springfield, Mother, forty years old, nearly lost her life due to complications during childbirth. Daddy pleaded with God in the hospital chapel through the long night of Michael's birth and death to let Mother live. God answered that prayer. She fully recovered physically but maybe never completely emotionally.

Daddy, though a good and honorable man, had never publicly made his profession of faith, and he made the decision that night that he wanted to. Very shortly after Michael's death, he along with Francie, Sherry, and I stood at the altar in the Old Stone Presbyterian Church, the first church built in Branson, as we all professed Jesus as our Savior. The four of us were baptized together. Our Sunday school, our church, and our faith were our pillars of strength during a sad time. Again, Romans 8:28 comes to mind as I reflect on the events of March 1958. Through the death of Michael, Daddy professed Jesus as his living Savior.

Among the most comforting of many letters Mother received during this time was one from Dr. R. M. Good, the longtime president of the School of the Ozarks, who had been a spiritual mentor and an inspiration to her during her time there as a high school student in the early 1930s. In his letter, twenty-five years after she graduated, he told her of the untimely death of his own young child and encouraged her to focus on her faith in God as her source of strength.

Attending Sunday school and church was as normal as breathing during my growing-up years. I am eternally thankful that God gave me parents who loved me enough to teach me about Him. I am thankful that Mother and Daddy both had parents who looked after the spiritual well-being of their children and instilled in them the desire to pass that heritage along to the next generation.

When the term *golden era* is used to describe a place, the implication is that it peaked at a certain point. This was especially true of Rockaway Beach. Its popularity peaked in the early 1960s, and its decline began in the 1970s and continued through the 1980s. It was a gradual decline brought about by several factors, including the completion of Table Rock Dam and the creation of a new vastly deep and magnificent recreational lake west of Branson. While providing much-needed flood control along the lakeside areas of Branson, Forsyth, and Rockaway, the new lake caused Lake Taneycomo to hover at a cool 56 degrees year round, as the cold water at the base of the dam was released there. Without the draw of its warm and gentle waters and the recreational sports they provided, tourism in Rockaway Beach was permanently and irreversibly damaged.

Then, the so-called riot in 1965 gained negative national media coverage, and Rockaway was saddled by television and newspapers with the reputation for being unsafe and no longer family-friendly. The people who experienced the event of July 4, 1965, know that it was nothing more than a small group of regional college students who had too much beer while celebrating the holiday at the Beach and got completely out of control. Francie and her then-husband, Bud, owned a gift shop on the main strip of the Beach. They had windows broken where students had thrown glass bottles, but there was no looting and no additional damage. Some local aspiring politicians seized the opportunity to make a name for themselves by trying to shine a negative light on the incident, but it was brief and a non-event to the locals.

Joan, in college at the time, was doing an internship with Senator Stuart Symington in Washington, DC, that year. On July 5, he read about the riot in Rockaway and called Joan into his office. He told her about it and suggested that she call her parents to see if they were okay. When she got them on the phone, Kenny did not know what they were talking about. He knew nothing about a riot, and he lived just half a block up the hill from the main strip of Rockaway Beach.

Some of the unruly beer-drinking college students were arrested for window-smashing and booked in the county jail, only to be released the next morning. The greatest damage to the business owners, which was significant and life-changing in some cases, was the loss of business for the rest of the 1965 season and subsequent seasons. The media portrayed the incident negatively. The story went nationwide through the Associated Press, and it frightened away longtime patrons to the point of not returning. Suffering from the loss of business, some business owners sold at deflated prices and others moved away. Effective leadership failed to emerge, as some of the founding families began to die. Rockaway Beach started to evolve into a different place, much different than it had been in its golden era.

In 2003, Kenny became ill and could no longer attend Sunday school. Attendance dwindled to Joan and one other member, Raylene. Faithfully, they continued attending each and every Sunday, mindful of the original charter and legal documents which stipulated that if the Sunday school ever ceased to be a church, the property and building would revert to the city. At the same time, an attempt to introduce gambling on Lake Taneycomo had sprung up, and Rockaway's city leaders were eager to get the resolution on the upcoming statewide ballot. They were aware of the documents that provided for the church property to revert to the city if the church closed its doors.

Raylene and Joan continued to meet and pray, seeking discernment as to what direction they should take. It was during this time that they contacted my husband and me and asked if we would join them in an effort to revive the Sunday school. We met with Joan and Raylene and felt called to do what we could to help.

One of the first steps we took was to make people at First Presbyterian in Branson, our church home, aware of the situation. Several of our church friends were eager to join us in Rockaway for a few walks through the neighborhood around the Sunday school, inviting residents for Sunday morning Bible study for people of all ages. We handed out flyers advertising a free breakfast before Sunday school, hoping that would attract families with young children. We had a few takers, but it was not a huge success. Still, volunteers from our church did some painting to freshen up the Sunday school building, and the joint efforts of Joan, Raylene, and willing members of First Presbyterian kept the doors open.

Meanwhile, the gambling initiative was growing, and city leaders made it known that they wanted the Sunday school building so they could tear it down and convert the property on which it sat to a parking lot for the gambling boat that would soon be operating on Lake Taneycomo. We ignored their comments and forged ahead. We had musicians on Sunday mornings who volunteered their time and talent, and our numbers began to grow. We continued to pray, because we had no idea where God was taking us on this journey. We made the effort to be there every Sunday morning to make pancakes and teach a children's and an adult's class, and that was as far ahead as we could discern.

After only a few months, we recognized that although there was a need in the community to keep our Sunday school alive, we were inadequate to lead it through a new era. Much to our surprise, we began getting phone calls from other ministries wanting information about the church, and within another few months, we had people from established churches in the area visiting us and sharing their vision for a church plant. Through these efforts, Bridge of Faith Community Church was conceived to reach the people of Rockaway Beach, a population that had changed slowly over a twenty-year period.

Coinciding with the new church plant, the gambling initiative was defeated in a statewide election, and the charter of 1953 providing for a church presence in Rockaway survived. Bridge of Faith Community Church, led now by Pastor Jonathan McQuire and his wife, Amy, reaches the unchurched, preaching the gospel of Jesus Christ, and enriching the lives of countless individuals who serve Him with their talent, time, and treasure. Bridge of Faith reaches out to more than two hundred children and adults for miles around the church who are bused in on Sunday morning and Wednesday evening for fellowship, food, and Bible study. The ministries of Bridge of Faith Community Church are changing lives in Rockaway Beach in a mighty and powerful way.

Once more, I reflect on Romans 8:28 (NIV): "And we know that in all things God works together for the good of those who love him and are called according to His purpose."

Easter Sunday

Swallowed up by thick fog, the three rough-hewn wooden crosses were barely visible on the shores of Lake Taneycomo. As we celebrated Jesus rising from the grave on Resurrection Sunday, the fog began to slowly lift, and the crosses emerged clearly as bundled-up worshippers sat at the foot of them in reverence and awe. They were reminded by the preacher of what had transpired more than two millennia earlier on the hill known as Golgotha outside of Jerusalem.

The celebration was attended by worshippers from all around the area, and early season tourists often made the pilgrimage to participate in the sacred experience. The sunrise service in Rockaway Beach was revered by residents, with more people attending that than any other church service of the year. The whole community rallied together to get the wooden crosses placed in the right spot on the grassy shores of the lake. Special music was arranged, and the piano and dozens of folding chairs were trucked down from the Sunday school building. One pickup load after another transported equipment and furniture to accommodate our residents and guests who attended.

After the early sunrise service, the men then moved everything back up the hill, and we had our own Bible study for children and adults during our normal Sunday school hour. It was a special day and a very busy one.

Around noon, a light-beige two-door Chevy Impala rolled into our driveway and parked in front of the stone bungalow. This was before we had moved to the big house. Mom, Daddy Dow, and Uncle Albert, their fourth child and only son, were joining us, as usual, for Easter Sunday dinner. They had attended the church service at their small country church in Brown Branch where the men sat on one side and the women on the other, or the men simply waited outside while the women attended.

Having quite the flare for entertaining, Mother could be counted upon to prepare lovely meals and had put the finishing touches on Easter dinner the night before. Eight of us, still dressed in our Easter Sunday clothes, sat on the blue-and-cream-striped upholstered chairs around the mahogany table in our small dining room. Mom, our very proper grandmother of English and Scottish descent, had on a spring navy blue dress and matching pillbox hat that sat elegantly atop her dark coiffed hair even as we ate. We girls were allowed to postpone changing into play clothes until after dinner because it was Easter Sunday.

As we dined on Mother's traditional Easter feast, basking in the company of family, we gazed out the windows at fresh blooms of redbud, dogwood, and lilacs as they were beginning to dot the landscape where our home and the cottages sat. Once the fog lifted and the day dried out, it was a beautiful Easter Sunday.

When the meal was finished, Mother's family had the habit of lingering around the dinner table. We girls listened to stories told by our mother and grandparents about family, friends, and neighbors who had been part of their lifelong community in eastern Taney County. The stories usually included who married whom, where they lived, and what they or their offspring were doing now. Sometimes the stories were funny; sometimes they were personal anecdotes about growing up in the Brown Branch area. In the era before television, computers, or iPads, much of a family's history was passed down around dining-room-table conversation.

Daddy, not having grown up in their part of the county, often did not know who the conversation was about, but he listened intently, and in all circumstances strove to treat Mom and Daddy

Dow with the greatest respect and courtesy. The stories often slightly bored me, but I was also fascinated by the tales of bygone times, people, and places. I found that I really enjoyed sitting around the table with them for prolonged periods of time wondering how one more story could top the last one.

Finally, with a break in the stories, Mother started clearing the plates so we could have dessert: the homemade strawberry shortcake she had prepared the day before. Usually, by Easter, fresh strawberries were available; they were stemmed, sugared, and mashed with an old-fashioned manual potato masher, creating a scrumptious topping for the one-egg cake that served as the base for Mother's version of this favorite family dessert. The cake was split into two pieces; the first was placed in the bowl with a spoonful of the strawberry mixture placed on top of it, then the second was added to that, followed by a second spoonful of strawberries. The best part was the dollop of freshly whipped cream on top.

Mother had always whipped her cream in an electric mixer, but the newly patented aerosol can of whipped cream called Reddi-wip had caught her attention and imagination. *How convenient it would be*, she thought, in a typical post–World War II mindset geared toward convenience, *if whipped cream as tasty as freshly whipped could be captured in a can*. She tried it and liked it. Not only did Mother like it, Daddy, always intrigued with new ideas, gadgets, and gimmicks, was completely taken by it.

As Mother served the strawberry shortcake without whipped cream so that each person could add his or her own, Daddy held the Reddi-wip can, eager to share their newfangled discovery with Mom and Daddy Dow, both born in the late nineteenth century and not accustomed to the conveniences of modern times. He looked at Mom and said, "Vera, you are going to love this! Let me put some whipped cream on your shortcake."

He took the can and began to place the dollop on my very prim and proper English grandmother's dessert … after which her face, her navy blue dress, and her matching pillbox hat were rapidly sprayed with a Reddi-wip aerosol can gone awry. Mother was aghast; Francie, Sherry, and I were stunned into silence; and poor Daddy became instantly pale. We didn't know what to expect next.

After a very pregnant pause, Mom decided the whipped cream was tasty. Mother gave her a cloth to help her clean her face. In between sweet smacks of fresh whipping cream, she said, "It's okay, Vernie! I know you didn't mean to do that!"

There were no hard feelings. Mom quickly got her wits back that Easter Sunday. She laughed and let Daddy off the hook for spraying her down with the newfangled contraption with which he had become seriously enamored. I saw that day that a sense of humor and not taking oneself too seriously can go a long way in promoting a healthy relationship with your daughter's husband.

Senior Trips

The lucky ones arrived in a Greyhound or a private charter bus. The others pulled up in a timeless yellow school bus with cheap vinyl seats and windows that, when lowered, provided natural air-conditioning. Either way, the mood among the wide-eyed seniors was rowdy, chattering, laughing, cutting up with their teachers and each other, and expecting to make memories with their classmates as they arrived in Rockaway Beach for the long-awaited high school senior trip. Some of the groups were small—fifteen students or less—but most were of fifty, seventy-five, or more.

During the fifties and sixties, senior trips were popular in the central part of the country. For some students, the trip to a place like Rockaway Beach provided a glimpse of what the world outside their hometown could offer. The farm communities in Kansas, Nebraska, Iowa, and northern Missouri were vastly different from the recreational areas of southwest Missouri, with its array of lakes and resort activities.

Upon arrival, the students were shown to their individual cottages, which Mother had determined long before they pulled into the driveway. When a busload or two of seniors began their descent onto the property, it took both Mother and Daddy to get them all where they needed to be. Mother had the procedure well organized and had corresponded by regular US postal service with the class sponsors for months during the fall and winter. Mother's list, handwritten on a stenographer's pad, noted which cottages were reserved for the girls and which for the boys. Individual names of students and chaperones staying in each cottage were arranged by the sponsors ahead of time, so it was just a matter of showing them where the cottages were. The settling-in process usually was completed within an hour after arrival, and then the fun began.

As an elementary student, I was impressed by these older students and had the feeling that I would never be as grown-up as they appeared to me. I envied the girls in their pastel-colored short shorts and pedal pushers and ruffled sissy blouses; their ponytails; and their saddle oxfords as they walked up and down the hills in pairs and groups. Swimming in the resort pool was one of the favorite daytime activities, along with horseback riding, go-carts, Skee-ball, and miniature golf.

The favorite nighttime activity was the dance pavilion or the Lake Queen. As I got older and was a high school student myself, it was great fun for Francie, Sherry, and I to meet up with Karen and Joan and go to the dance pavilion and dance for a few hours in the screened-in building. By selecting a table, getting a glass-bottled Coke with a straw, and perusing the dance floor, we were tacitly announcing that we were available to dance. The visitors to the Beach were a little intrigued by the locals, and we didn't sit out too many forty-fives. Buddy Holly's "Maybe, Baby" had a beat that was too irresistible to ignore and generated an uncontrollable eagerness to get onto the dance floor.

Introductions often occurred during the first dance. Sometimes there was a second dance with the same individual, sometimes not. It really was about the music. The screening around the perimeter of the dance pavilion building kept the mosquitoes out but let the humidity in. As we fed dimes and quarters into the jukebox, we did the jitterbug to songs like "Wake Up Little Susie," or "Blue Suede Shoes," and as perspiration beaded on our foreheads, we sported a natural moisture glow. Thankfully, "The Great Pretender" by the Platters or "Chances Are" by Johnny Mathis would come on, and we could slow dance and recoup from the more strenuous jitterbug.

Weekends would beckon us to the popular Lake Queen with its trusty paddle wheel for the nine-mile cruise down Lake Taneycomo to Branson on the open-air dance floor. For this excursion, we had not only humidity to deal with but fog so thick it was sometimes hard to recognize a face only three feet away. The moisture, thick in the air from humidity and fog, did not deter us from an outing on the Lake Queen. It was fun to meet people our own age from other places, dance with them, and hear about their impressions of Rockaway Beach and their comparisons of our town to theirs.

We heard about farm towns, small towns, and good-sized cities, and what life was like in those places so unfamiliar to our little group of siblings and friends who had been born in Rockaway Beach and never imagined leaving its safe, sweet, small-town city limits to live anywhere else. Friendships were occasionally formed that resulted in some letter-writing and picture exchanges for a while after the visitors had gone home, but mostly we looked forward to April and May of the next year to meet a whole new crop of seniors who came to Rockaway Beach.

It never occurred to me that this was an unusual way to spend warm spring days and nights—meeting people from other places and learning about their schools, their families, and their friends and circumstances, all the while gaining a new perspective on this place we called home. Having hundreds of new and interesting teenagers descend upon our little town every spring was all I had ever known. It was like the changing of the seasons: normal and completely predictable. As the senior trips came to an end around Memorial Day, honeymooners and more quiet and sedate families started arriving in June, and summer was upon us.

A White Rose

On Mother's Day when I was five, Daddy went to the rosebushes on the east side of our little stone house and cut four red roses and one white rose. The idea of wearing a white rose made me sad. On Mother's Day, Daddy reminded us with a white rose in the lapel of his double-breasted suit that his mother was no longer living. It made me sad that he no longer had a mother and that Francie, Sherry, and I had no mother of our daddy who we could call Grandma. She had died before any of us was born, and we felt that void in our young lives.

Daddy often shared stories of his mother, Ethel Rebecca, but especially on Mother's Day. He told of how hard she worked on the Michel Homestead to raise her brood of twelve children, burying precious little Ella before the child turned three years old. Daddy believed that hard work and grief were the cause of her very premature death at age fifty-two. He loved and admired her, spoke of her often, and conveyed to us what an amazing woman she was, raising her family in a humble roughly hewn log cabin with no running water, no electricity, and only a horse-drawn wagon for transportation.

Our maternal grandmother, Vera Reese, Mom, was part of our lives until we reached adulthood and became mothers ourselves. She, too, worked hard on the family farm to raise her five children and to feed and sometimes house hired help who were often there during the summer and fall months. Having a distinct aristocratic countenance about her, Mom was well-educated and refined. Her father, Great-Grandpa Albert Dean, was a successful cattle rancher in eastern Taney County in the late 1800s and the early twentieth century. He provided a beautiful two-story Victorian home and many advantages for his three daughters, including college, musical training, and travel as they were growing up in the tiny rural hamlet of Brown Branch.

Mom was a positive influence in my life with her wisdom, her intellect, and her sense of English propriety handed down to my own mother and to my sisters and me. As a very young girl, I felt comforted on Mother's Day to see that homegrown red rose pinned to my own dear mother's Sunday dress to honor her mother and my grandmother.

Pampered by Daddy year after year, the red and white rosebushes just below our dining room window produced an abundance of fragrant blossoms from which to choose on the second Sunday in May. It was Daddy's job to select the roses and cut one for Mother, my sisters, and me. On this particular Mother's Day, Francie, Sherry, and I were decked out for Sunday school in pink-dotted Swiss dresses with large frilly collars; black patent leather shoes with white ankle socks; straw hats adorned with colorful cloth flowers; and white gloves. At the very last minute before leaving the house, Daddy ceremoniously brought in the clipped roses and presented them to us with as much pride as if he had purchased them from the finest purveyor of flowers. Mother pinned them to our dresses, and our family walked up the hill to Sunday school.

I had a sense of joy on Mother's Day knowing that I had a precious mommy who loved me, and she still had hers. When Kenny said the opening prayer, Daddy's white rose made me want to take his hand, squeeze it, and tell him how sorry I was that he didn't have his mother. I also wanted him to know how much I loved him and how thankful I was to be sitting beside him in Sunday school on Mother's Day.

Bull Creek

"Yea! Yea! Yea! We get to go!"

The excitement in our voices said it all. We were full, and Mother and Daddy guardedly agreed that it might be a good day to go to the creek. *Full* meant that all the cottages were rented and all the guests had arrived and checked in. We hung the wooden *No Vacancy* sign from the bottom of our permanent green maple-leaf-shaped Michel's Court sign at the entrance to the cottages. On those magical summer afternoons before we had our own swimming pool, when we got the same good news from the Puchtas and Schneikarts (close friends and neighboring business owners who always went with us), we gleefully anticipated an afternoon of fun, swimming, and eating at our favorite summertime swimming hole: Bull Creek in Walnut Shade.

Mother, Francie, Sherry, and I climbed into the back of the '52 aqua Chevy pickup truck that Daddy had outfitted with old-fashioned wooden spring wagon seats he'd repurposed from the lawn furniture dotted throughout the resort landscape. There were three rows of authentic wooden spring seats placed on top of notched log planks that held them securely in the back of the pickup. We settled in with Daddy in the cab of the truck heading to the neighbors' courts.

The long-held tradition among the three families decreed that we go as a group. If one of the three resorts was not full, plans for the creek didn't stand a chance; but on a rare day with all conditions just right, we tried hard to make it happen. On especially hot days, Francie, Joan, and I monitored the *Vacancy* signs at all three resorts, and as soon as all three had their *No Vacancy* signs up, our black rotary phones began ringing in a steady back and forth as we pleaded with the parents to put together a swimming trip to Bull Creek. Finally, one of the three or four days during the summer would fall into place, and we'd put a handwritten sign on the office door that read, "Gone to the creek. Back around 9."

As we arrived at the Puchtas, out came Hazel, Kenny, ponytailed Joan, and little brother Ken, carrying their baskets of food. Kenny hopped in the cab of the truck with Daddy, and the others found a place on the wagon seats. We then headed on down the hill toward the lake to pick up the Schneikart family and Karen at Captain Bill's Hotel. Then we'd backtrack up the big hill away from the Beach and toward the creek. Usually, as we left the Beach, we wanted to drive along the lake so we could see the swimmers, paddleboats, and all the hustle and bustle taking place during the busy summer season. When headed to the creek, however, we didn't want to waste a precious moment getting there.

Excited as eager little kindergartners on the first day of school, anticipating the fun and adventure awaiting us along the rocky banks of Bull Creek, we girls chattered incessantly during the short ride, so proud that we had put the adventure together. We had three happy daddies in the cab enjoying their freedom from the babble of three moms and seven kids riding on old-fashioned wagon spring seats in the back of the pickup truck, all of us oblivious to the notion that we might look just a little odd to cars behind us or meeting us on the two-lane winding highway that led to our remote destination in the countryside.

On those warm summer afternoons, the blazing sun hammered us as we left ourselves completely exposed to its burning rays during the late afternoon ride. If sunscreen was available, we hadn't discovered it, but sufficiently lathered in baby oil or Coppertone, we didn't give the intense heat a second thought, knowing the misery would subside as soon as we got wet. The horseshoe curve just outside Walnut Shade told us we were almost there, and excitement built.

I tried not to think about the sharp, jagged creek rocks I'd have to step on as I made my way to the gentle ripples awaiting me. My seven-year-old lifetime of experiences told me it was the price I had to pay to get to the water. I had not yet felt the soft, squishy sand of coastal beaches, so I had nothing to compare to the rocky banks of Taney County swimming holes. I'm quite sure I would not have been so fond of going to the creek if I had known that some folks swam on white sandy beaches and never had to endure the piercing pain of native rocks on bare feet.

Oh, the ecstasy of jumping into the sparkling water! I stayed in the shallow part because I was not yet a swimmer. I wanted to learn, and Daddy was determined that I would learn, so he had me lie on my tummy, and he held the straps of my swimming suit to keep me afloat. A certified Red Cross instructor he was not! His method of teaching swimming didn't work, nor did it prevent me from loving those afternoons and evenings playing with my favorite people in all the world. Francie and Sherry, Karen, Joan, and I, plus the two little guys, Ken and George Earl, along with the grown-ups, splashed and played for hours. We swung from a rope tied to a tree and did modified cannonballs into shallow water, always on the lookout for the water moccasin, black, or cottonmouth snakes that occasionally wanted to invade our swimming hole.

After a few hours of swimming, hunger pangs began to run rampant, so we eagerly unpacked the homemade picnic that Mother and the two Hazels had effortlessly whipped up in just a couple of hours. The menu was always the same: fried chicken, baked beans, deviled eggs, potato salad, chocolate cake, and bread-and-butter sandwiches cut into four even squares for easy eating. As dusk crept upon us, we roasted marshmallows and began to think about returning home. If any among us wanted to change from a wet swimming suit to dry clothes, we had to find a bush or tree large enough to provide privacy, because the creek bank offered no restrooms. Walking on the rocks and gravel in bare feet, struggling with a tight-fitting swimming suit while squatting behind a bush and looking out for snakes lurking underfoot created an environment that made even squeamish little girls pretty gutsy!

Hot and sticky and sad for the day to end, we piled back into the pickup. In spite of the warm evening, we were a little chilled from our damp clothes, wet towels, and the evening breeze pounding our faces and hair as we headed home in our open-air limousine. Tired and spent from the activities of the day, we were quiet compared to the ride there. The twenty-minute ride back to the Beach provided an opportunity to reflect on the adventures of the afternoon. It was fun! It was a time to be with family and friends. We enjoyed our feast of good homemade food spread on a cotton tablecloth on the rocky bank of Bull Creek.

Without a care in the world, we already looked forward to a repeat of the same summer adventure. As we approached the turnoff to get to our homes the shorter back way, we seven kiddos proudly sitting on the wagon seats began our chant to Daddy in the cab of the truck, "Go through the Beach! Go through the Beach!"

The three mamas in the back of the truck, all recognized as pillars of the community, sitting on 1880s wagon spring seats, wet hair matted to their scalps and in creek clothes attire, said to themselves and each other, "No! We are not Fibber McGee and Molly!" They knew every time what to expect, and they knew that the delightful pleas of the seven little ones in the back of the '52 aqua-green pickup would somehow transcend their concerns about looking a bit backward and unsophisticated.

Maybe reluctantly, maybe expectantly, the daddies always took us through the Beach, where we got plenty of smiles and waves from friends, neighbors, and sophisticated city-folk tourists who may have secretly envied the locals so obviously enjoying a warm, starlit summer Ozarks night, unabashedly proud at that moment to claim the title of *hillbilly*. The ride through the Beach was the perfect ending to a perfect afternoon.

What a day! Little did I know at that young age that I was making memories that would last a lifetime.

The Skillman Family

Cottage number ten was spic-and-span clean. The linoleum floors were mopped, waxed, and shiny, and a fresh bouquet of flowers from Mother's big flower garden bordered with native fieldstone sat in the middle of the red chrome table in the cottage's small eating area. We girls anxiously watched for the late-model Olds with Texas license plates to pull into the driveway of Michel's Cottage Court. It happened every July like clockwork. Francie, Sherry, and I were excited to see our friends Sue Ella, a year older than Francie, and her little sister, Carol, who was smack-dab between Sherry and me in age.

During the early years of their visits to the Ozarks, the Skillmans stayed in cottage number ten with its two separate bedrooms, one bathroom, and a kitchen and eating area completely equipped for housekeeping with percolator coffeepot, toaster, pots and pans, and authentic multicolored Fiesta Ware. The front porch had screens all around covered with sturdy windows that could be opened; the cool night temperatures required a light sheet or blanket for sleeping. The mating sound of the nocturnal katydids, phoneticized rhythmically to sound like, "katy-did, katy-didn't," was known to lull some folks to sleep. Because of the heavy foliage on the tall oak, maple, and walnut trees on our property, these little creatures were an enduring part of the Ozark hills nighttime experience.

With the need to have windows open for sleeping during the heat of summer, the symphony of the katydids was not a choice. They were ever-present. Toward the mid-fifties, when air-conditioning was installed in the cottages, it did become a choice when folks took advantage of the extra creature comfort it afforded. They were willing to plunk a handful of quarters into the window unit to get eight hours of air-conditioned sleep. Yep, that's right—a clunky metal box attached to the window air-conditioning unit took enough quarters at one time for up to eight hours of uninterrupted slumber.

The Skillman family, coming from Port Arthur, Texas, liked our milder Ozark Mountain summer temperatures, and they chose to sleep with their windows open. Sue Ella, Carol, Christine (or Chris), and "Skillet" rarely used the air-conditioning during their two-week stay in the Ozarks, raving about the refreshing cooler climate and lower humidity than they lived with in their Texas hometown. Once we moved into our new home, we converted our little rock bungalow into a rental; it became number fourteen, and after many years of staying in number ten, the family decided to try number fourteen. They loved it, and it became their new favorite for more than ten years until Sue Ella and Carol were out of high school.

When the Skillmans arrived, usually around midday, Mother and Daddy somehow managed, even while taking care of the business, to have a meal prepared. Daddy set up two grills and made barbecued chicken along with kraut-filled and bacon-wrapped hot dogs. Mother orchestrated the rest of the meal, adding fresh sliced tomatoes, Mom Reese's cut-off-the-cob creamed corn, hot buttered and garlic French bread, and peach or blackberry cobbler. The two families, with Ed in a highchair, gathered around the big yellow chrome and Formica table with matching chairs for the Skillman family welcoming party.

Looking back on those times, I marvel that Mother and Daddy were able to produce such a feast while managing the resort, but then I recall that they didn't do it alone. They had Francie, Sherry, and me helping in the kitchen from a very early age. During the summer especially, we learned how to peel and slice tomatoes, cut corn off the cob, peel peaches, and set the table correctly with the fork on the left, the knife with its rounded side facing the right side of the plate, and the spoon to the right of the knife.

We were trained from the same early age to clean up the kitchen. We had no garbage disposal, so cleaning up meant scraping all of the leftovers into one large container and dumping it into the garbage can in the garage. It sat beside a larger container that held paper and dry trash, and a service disposed of it once a week. Francie, being the oldest, usually was willing to dump the garbage because she knew how much I despised that chore, but to taunt me, she could be counted on to complain to Mother that "Marilyn will never take out the garbage. I have to always do it." Nevertheless, she was a good big sister.

When the welcoming meal was over and the kitchen cleaned up, we were free to play with Sue Ella and Carol. Skillet recruited help from all the girls to get the car unloaded, and Chris directed the settling in. The whole process was done in a jiffy, and we five girls were off to the Beach.

With its eclectic conglomeration of businesses, the Beach was a vacation paradise for all ages. The array of activities was bountiful. Among the most popular was horseback riding. Two small family-owned businesses provided horseback-riding trips: Hugh and Bob's Stables on one side of the Beach and Charlie and Don's on the other. They rode lakeside with a small flip spiral notebook and pencil in the front pocket of their Western-style shirts soliciting customers for rides that took place on the hour all day long. A reservation was made verbally and written down in the small notebook, which was then tucked back into the shirt pocket.

Hugh and Bob's was the long-standing favorite of Sue Ella and Carol, and the stable helpers remembered them from year to year. When we were spotted strolling the Beach, plans were put into place for a riding trip. Our favorite rides were the three-hour-long breakfast ride in the morning and the swimming ride in the afternoon. Eighteen-year-old Billy Thurman—a nephew of the owner, Bob, and one of the ranch hands taking care of the horses—gave us special attention because Sue Ella batted her pretty brown eyes at him. I saw some serious flirting going on between them for a couple of weeks every July.

The popular breakfast ride began early in the morning. Alarms were set for five thirty, and we expected to be picked up around six in a specially outfitted pickup truck. Riders climbed up into the truck and sat on benches attached to both sides of the truck bed as it made its way to all of the cottages up and down the hills of the Beach where riders needed to be picked up. When the benches filled up, the last few guests rode tailgate with their feet hanging down as the group slowly wound its way to the stables.

The early-morning hours offered a fresh perspective on the Beach for some folks; it was quiet and peaceful, birds were chirping, and fog was rising on the lake. Few people were out and about. Perhaps an occasional proprietor was seen sweeping a sidewalk or getting other chores done before the day began. It took about an hour to get to the stables, climb out of the truck, and get mounted on the gentle, well-trained horses.

Starting out around seven o'clock, the breakfast trip riders meandered their way for an hour through uninhabited, densely treed hills, going east several miles toward a country restaurant near Forsyth. Once there, the riders dismounted and tied their horses to a rail fence, went in, had a hearty breakfast, then returned the same way along the trails. They were delivered back to the cottages by around ten o'clock in the same way they were picked up. The Skillman girls loved the horses and often took a little nap after the breakfast ride so they could be picked up at noon to take the Bull Creek ride. Sometimes we went with them all day, sometimes we didn't.

The Bull Creek ride began at one in the afternoon. It was an hour ride through the trails west to Bull Creek where it intersected with the White River. Guests usually wore their swimming suits under their clothes; if they didn't, they had to change behind a bush or tree for privacy. The Bull Creek ride took patrons to a different area of Bull Creek than our family went to in Walnut Shade, but all the same, there were no restrooms.

When the water was high in the creek, the horses had to wade through it. Water covered the riders up to the horse's saddle. Perhaps this was why we wore shorts and tennis shoes on these trips rather than jeans and boots. The likelihood of having wet legs and feet even before we got to the swimming hole was strong.

After swimming for an hour in the shimmering, clear water of the creek, we returned along the same trails and were delivered back home by four o'clock. Doing two rides in one day was unusual for us, except when the Skillmans were in town. They loved the horses. One day, Carol did something to startle one of the horses, and she got a good horse nip on her leg. Even that unusual bit of aggression didn't keep her from getting back up on the saddle, though, with only a minor bruise on her leg. According to little sister Sherry, her riding mate during the incident, Chris and Skillet saw no need to seek medical help.

All the cottages on the Beach were within walking distance of the lake and its endless activities. Our parents were comfortable with us going to the recreational boat docks alone, where we took out nonmotorized paddle boats. They were powered by foot and leg motion, and as junior high students, we reveled in this kind of independence. Wisely, life jackets were required, and we complied.

The owners of all the businesses kept an eye on the locals. They were friends with Mother and Daddy, so if we were up to something, our parents would hear about it sooner rather than later. Chris and Skillet rarely accompanied their daughters to the Beach to participate in the kid-friendly activities that we never tired of—Skee-ball, miniature golf, bowling, or bumper cars—because it was a safe environment and we roamed in small groups. Chris and Skillet did not come to Rockaway to be on the go for two weeks, and they appreciated that the girls could safely come and go. They were clear about the reason they came, and that was to rest and relax in their beloved number ten and eventually number fourteen cottage.

One enchanting spot that lured many guests to get behind the wheel of their car and venture two miles from the Beach up the steep Cedar Point hill was Taneycomo Country Club in Forsyth. Occasionally, Mother, Daddy, Francie, Sherry, and I accompanied the Skillmans to the country club, and both families spent the evening hitting golf balls from the driving range, having dinner, and dancing under the stars. The public golf club was a favorite of tourists and locals alike. During my growing-up years, my cousin Karen's grandparents, who lived in Forsyth, often took us to the club, where we met up with Joe Hall and Jackie Pulley, some of our Forsyth friends. We roamed freely from the restaurant to the driving range to the open-air dance arena adorned with glittering lights, which featured live musicians and family-friendly fun under the bright moon and brilliant stars of an Ozark summer night. It was rare that my parents left the resort on a summer evening, but one of my favorite childhood memories is of watching them dance at Taneycomo Country Club to one of their favorite songs, "The Tennessee Waltz."

Many of our guests, as the saying goes, "came as strangers and left as friends." But the bond between our two families made the Skillmans' friendship extraordinary. After many consecutive years of spending their coveted two-week vacation away from their furniture store in Port Arthur, the family decided that they should try a different destination. They heard from their furniture-store customers and others that Hawaii was the "dream vacation," so they didn't come to Rockaway one year but went to Hawaii for two weeks. The next summer, when they arrived back in the Ozarks, they said, "Nope, that was not for us!" They spent many subsequent vacations in Rockaway Beach at Michel's Cottage Court, enjoying their home in the hills.

The Skillmans watched Michel's Cottage Court evolve in the late fifties to Michel's Court, then to Michel's Motor Lodge in the sixties, and finally to Michel's of the Ozarks in the seventies and eighties. Even with the updating of our resort name, we never abandoned the slogan "Follow the Leaves to Your Home in the Hills" or what it represented. Comfort for our guests was a top priority, and it brought many guests, like the Skillmans, back year after year.

Because we operated a summer resort, our family did not take summer vacations, but we did take fall trips. Mother and Daddy tried to coordinate them with the two or three days we were out of school in the autumn for teachers' meetings. Even if we missed a week or ten days of school, we traveled in October, usually through the South. With Daddy in his suit, tie, and wide-brimmed hat and Mother in her two-piece suit with silk blouse, high heels, and stockings, we would take off for a road trip with no particular destination in mind. Daddy loved to visit state capitols and made it a point to tour capitol buildings when we were close to one, but a planned agenda was not appealing to him as a traveler. Rather, he enjoyed driving, and if we found an interesting site to explore, we would stop and look around. He didn't care if we only traveled fifty miles in a day. If we saw places of interest, it was a good day.

One year, we planned a rather ambitious trip. Daddy and Uncle, along with Mother and Auntie, determined that it would be fun for both families to take a trip together. Their family and ours, along with Grandpa Michel—twelve altogether—embarked upon a two-week trip to Texas, Louisiana, the Carolinas, and Florida. This trip had a planned destination. We were going to Port Arthur to visit the Skillmans for Thanksgiving, then on to New Orleans to sightsee, and to Pensacola, Florida, to visit Aunt Libby and Uncle Bert, then to North and South Carolina. Each leg of the trip was planned to accommodate the large traveling group, but restaurants were chosen as the need arose. Our most substantial meal of the day was the noon meal, and in the evening we ate lightly.

One evening in the New Orleans area, we pulled into a restaurant, and the twelve of us went into a cafeteria. We saw a bountiful line of beautifully prepared food, served in what we knew as cafeteria-style, where we selected what we wanted and paid for each selection of food individually. Both sets of parents reminded us that we were to be prudent in our selections and eat lightly. We followed their example as they carefully chose one or two items from the cafeteria line for their light evening meal.

After finishing the meal, we got a surprise when we went to pay. We learned a new word that day that we hadn't been exposed to in Taney County: *smorgasbord*. The price we were charged for each individual was a set amount regardless of what we consumed. Our prudence was for nothing. We could have enjoyed a lovely feast that evening, but we didn't.

Not long after this unforgettable experience, we saw that word popping up in places all over Taney County. Within a year, Uncle Lee—another of the Michel boys who caught the attention of Captain Bill Roberts and was now the operating manager of Captain Bill's Hotel—had created an amazing smorgasbord buffet at the restaurant there. It didn't take long for the popularity of that restaurant concept to spread across the country.

As we traveled through the countryside of North Carolina with Auntie, Uncle, and the cousins, we saw signs advertising Cherokee Village. We had stopped at this roadside attraction a few years earlier, and Francie, Sherry, and I had gotten Indian dolls dressed in buckskin clothes and moccasins. Daddy promised we could stop again when we got there. Browsing through the aisles of the gift shop, we bumped into the Schneikart family, also enjoying a fall getaway through the South. They had decided on a whim to take a trip, and we weren't aware of their plans. Imagine the sweet serendipity of running into your best friends and neighbors 750 miles from home in 1953 when you were least expecting it.

The Skillmans were gracious hosts when our small army of people invaded them for Thanksgiving that year. It was a special experience to visit our longtime guests on their turf. We toured their town, saw where the girls went to school, and visited Skillman's Furniture Store, which we had heard so much about over the years. They continued their journeys to Rockaway Beach until the girls were grown, and when she was fifteen years old, Sherry went home with them one summer and stayed three weeks. Lovely people, lovely times, lovely memories! They came as guests, they left as friends.

My First Work Experiences

The summer I turned ten, Daddy had a bright idea. He sat me down one day and said, "Marilyn Jeanie, how would you like to earn your own money this summer?"

Not quite sure what he was thinking, I asked him to tell me how he thought I might do that, and he explained that I could help the ladies who cleaned the cottages. From as early as I can remember, we girls liked to tag along with Ruth, Sadie, and Pauline as they were in and out of the cottages daily. Patiently, they allowed us to help, and they asked us to make little runs to the storeroom to retrieve a forgotten item, so it was an appealing idea to get paid for doing something I wanted to be doing.

Daddy struck a deal with me that summer to pay me one dollar for every bed I made. He told me to keep track of it, and he would pay me right before Labor Day. I was thrilled at the idea of having my own money, and I took the offer seriously.

We didn't have golf carts to carry us around the property. Ruth, Sadie, and Pauline, in their pink polyester uniforms, walked thousands of steps among the fifteen cottages, day after day, making sure they were in that spic-and-span condition the Skillmans and all the other guests expected. Daddy put me under the direct supervision of these three valued employees who were also, because of their longevity with our family, precious friends.

I learned all the necessary steps to gather linens for the beds. What I especially loved was selecting the perfect chenille bedspread to fit the color scheme of each cottage. Mother did not buy the bedspreads from large commercial supply houses; rather, she ordered each one from Sears and Roebuck or Montgomery Ward catalogs. Always attentive to detail, she coached me at the beginning of the day to use specific bedspreads in specific cottages. The popular chenilles, in their array of assorted colors and flower patterns, contributed to the cozy homespun effect our guests enjoyed.

Well before fitted sheets were available, I learned from our cleaning ladies how to make a bed with military precision. Both sheets had to be mitered to a ninety-degree angle on both sides of the bed and pulled as tight as possible so no wrinkles were visible when the bed was made. After the sheets were carefully placed, the bedspread was placed so that it hung proportionately on each side and was turned down slightly at the head of the bed. I then placed the tip of the pillow under my chin and pulled the pillow case on, smoothed it, and laid it flat on the bed. Placing my arm in the middle of each pillow, I formed each one into a perfect roll and placed it carefully above the turned-down sheets. Finally, I was taught to cover the pillows with the bedspread so that the two pillows at the top of the bed gave the appearance of being one long roll. This was how our ladies were trained by Mother to make the beds, and they lovingly helped me redo if it didn't meet their standards.

I eventually got the hang of it, and as the summer progressed, I learned the importance of keeping good records. Each day as I finished my work in the cottages, I recorded the number of beds I'd made. By summer's end, I had made one hundred beds, and Daddy gave me a crisp one hundred dollar bill.

Mother and Daddy helped me open my first bank account with that one hundred dollars, and I used the money during the school year to buy Christmas presents for the family and other things I wanted. I learned how to write a check and to make deductions in my checkbook. For some reason, I kept my checkbooks over the years and found it amusing that I regularly wrote a check for one, two, or three dollars for purchases. The hundred dollars was ample for my spending money for a whole school year. It gave me a great deal of satisfaction to know that I had earned it.

Once I experienced that little taste of financial independence gained through making beds, I was motivated to try something a bit more demanding and financially rewarding. Uncle Lee and Aunt Virginia were the longtime managers of Captain Bill's Hotel, and Karen was already working a few hours in the coffee shop waiting tables. They asked me if I wanted to try it. Of course, they were family, so Mother and Daddy agreed to let me give it a try.

The next summer, at the age of eleven, I had my first job under the watchful eye of my aunt and uncle. They were kind and protective, and the clientele was mostly families. I was trained on how to take care of customers. Uncle Lee was the chef and one of the hardest-working people I have ever been around. He was up at five in the morning to prepare pastries for breakfast, worked through breakfast and lunch, took a few hours off around one in the afternoon, and returned at four to do all of the cooking through the dinner hour until ten or eleven at night. The coffee shop and dining room were both open all of these hours and, combined, were able to serve up to 175 guests at a time. Uncle Lee had helpers in the kitchen, but he assumed the responsibility for getting all of the orders prepared and ready to serve.

Before the age of computers, it was customary in a restaurant to see orders written down and mounted on a spindle for the chef to rotate as he prepared food orders. Uncle Lee, however, had no such device. His method of remembering an order was simply to repeat it back to the waitress who called it out in the first place. The entrees offered multiple options, usually a choice of baked potato, mashed potatoes, or French fries, and a selection of several vegetables. Once he called it back successfully to the waitress, it was ingrained in his memory until he placed it on the shelf to be served. He rarely made a mistake, even when the house was full.

I worked for Uncle Lee and Aunt Virginia for several summers, from the time I was about eleven until I was about fourteen. I learned the meaning of hard work, for which I am grateful. Waiting tables is not easy, and the hours we were expected to work would not be allowed for young people today. A normal shift was from seven in the morning to one in the afternoon, off for four or five hours, and then back to the restaurant for the evening shift from five to ten.

Captain Bill's Hotel was popular with families, and for the most part, when people are vacationing, they are pleasant to work with. I learned patience from those who weren't pleasant, and I have never forgotten what that kind of service work entails. I appreciate people who work in the service industry because of my experiences as a very young person who learned how to handle a grown-up's job.

When I entered high school, I decided that I wanted a change from Captain Bill's Hotel. Francie had worked for Bud Naioti all through high school, and she made what I thought were better tips—which was, of course, our reason for working in a restaurant. So, the summer after my freshman year, I began working at Naioti's Italian Restaurant. It was much smaller than Captain Bill's but equally popular. Over a summer, Francie and I could each make as much as $1,500 in tips, and like squirrels stash away acorns for the long winter months in the Ozarks, we stashed our summer earnings away in our bank accounts.

I learned the value of saving and managing my money, I learned how to get along in the workplace with different types of personalities, and I learned the importance of commitment. I understood that when I told Uncle Lee or Bud Naioti that I would be there at a certain time, they were counting on me. Both were astute businessmen, and they had high expectations.

One very busy evening during the dinner hour when I was about fifteen, I waited on a table of four. They all ordered the same chicken-fried steak meal, each meal costing one dollar and fifty cents. Drinks and salad were included in that price, so it was a simple ticket to calculate. Again, before computers or calculators, all figuring had to be done using basic math skills. In my haste to take care of my load of customers, I figured the ticket for four dinners at one dollar and fifty cents each and wrote total due as four dollars and fifty cents. This customer was not honest. He paid the four dollars and fifty cents and left.

When Bud took a closer look at the ticket, he realized my mistake, and at the end of the evening, he asked to talk to me. He showed me the ticket and confronted me with my mistake. I recognized my error, apologized for my carelessness, and offered to pay the one dollar and fifty cents difference from my tips. He thought about it for a minute, and then he said firmly, "I won't have you pay me back this time, but if it happens again, I will."

Bud Naioti was a good man to work for. He was fair, and he was kind, but he taught me that I had to carry my own weight, and that mistakes come with a consequence. I'm thankful for that teaching.

In spite of the long hours and the responsibilities of a summer job, there was plenty of time for fun. My friend Joe Hall had a speedboat from the time he was able to drive one. A group of us would meet most afternoons at the boat docks and ski the wonderfully warm and calm waters of Lake Taneycomo. Astonishingly, our parents allowed us to go out on the lake without adult supervision throughout our high school years. We spent many, many hours cruising the lake and skiing. We challenged ourselves and each other to ski the nine miles from the docks in Rockaway to the docks in Branson without falling. That was our goal, and we did it countless times during the summer months. Most of us had jobs to get back to, so sunburned but energized, we went back to work, looking forward to the next afternoon on the lake to do it all over again.

A strong work ethic was instilled in me by my parents at a young age, as it had been instilled in them by their parents. I have no regrets about working at such a young age. In the twenty-first century, child labor laws would prohibit children from working as my sisters and I did. I never felt mistreated; on the contrary, I felt protected, because I was under the care and scrutiny of close family and friends who had high expectations along with nurturing hearts. They valued a strong work ethic and wanted to pass it along to future generations. What a precious gift it was to be taught the value of work!

Daddy always told us as we were growing up that one should never be embarrassed or shamed by any kind of work as long as it was honest. Those words have stayed with me all my life, and remembering them has made it possible for me to look at people who do honest work that could be perceived as insignificant, trivial, or paltry, and find it in my heart to admire and appreciate their effort, industry, and willingness to work rather than not work when they needed to.

Dr. and Mrs. Frost

Catty-corner across the street from the schoolhouse, tucked into the woods at the foot of the big hill going west out of the Beach, sat a large circa-1940s home similar in Ozark giraffe rock style to the bungalow we lived in until 1954, when we moved to our big house. Dr. Ralph W. Frost, a retired dentist from Kansas City, and his wife, Ethel, built their home and moved to Rockaway Beach to escape the pressures of the big city and the responsibilities of a busy dental practice. They chose not to get involved in community activities, but they were respected, accepted, and loved by residents of the Beach.

They didn't want to participate in city government or civic and volunteer activities, but they loved children. They loved inviting the children of the Beach into their home, and they had an open-door invitation to the children at any time of the day. During the summer months, when we had no school, it wasn't unusual for Karen and me to knock on their door, unexpectedly, as early as ten o'clock in the morning. They always gave us a warm welcome and invited us in. Looking back, I wonder how they were so flexible to stop whatever they were doing to play games or do puzzles with any number of children showing up on a whim at their front door.

There was an aura about both the doctor and his wife that fascinated me. Mrs. Frost was always dressed and ready to greet guests morning, noon, and night. Her silver hair was pulled loosely in a bun, with a few strands dangling down each side of her gently freckled face. Her blushed cheeks were natural, and her porcelain-like face showed no hint of lipstick or mascara. Her natural look matched her natural ability to engage children in an easy and comfortable manner.

I don't recall asking her or Dr. Frost when we barged in unexpectedly if they wanted to spend a few hours visiting with us or playing games or puzzles, but we never were turned away. They asked us about our friends, our school activities, and our hopes and dreams for the future. They encouraged us to stay involved in wholesome activities like Sunday school, church, and sports, and made every boy and girl who walked through that door believe in themselves and believe that they could make positive contributions to mankind.

Dr. Frost, an avid reader, encouraged me to read and write and dream big dreams. He inquired about books I was reading and engaged me in conversation about the characters, setting, and plot in a way that didn't make me feel like I was being quizzed by a teacher. I learned from our conversations that he was a ghostwriter. He explained what that meant, and I wondered as a young teen why anyone would want to write for someone else rather than take credit for himself. He introduced a new concept to me, one of many that I attribute to my doctor friend.

The interior walls of the house were light pine throughout the living area, dining room, and sparsely equipped kitchen—in contrast to our kitchen, which was stocked with every gadget imaginable. I marveled that a meal could be produced with the limited equipment visible. I was convinced that this elderly couple must not eat anything at all, because there was no way it could be prepared in a kitchen with no equipment. The seating in the living room was made up of hand-hewed pine chairs and sofas upholstered with durable, heavy, earth-toned fabrics. The chairs, sofas, and end tables with minimal accessories surrounded a large stone fireplace.

It was, however, not the living room where we usually gathered with the doctor and his wife. As we entered the house, they would lead us into the separate dining room with its large round pine table and chairs. It had a matching hutch that housed assorted games, puzzles, cards, and several sets of blocks with paper coverings that created a picture when put together correctly. It was the latter that enamored me as a young child, and when I graduated high school, they gifted me with that set of blocks that created scenes from Little Red Riding Hood, The Three Little Pigs, Snow White, and Cinderella when turned exactly the right way. I treasured that gift and eventually passed it on to my children and grandchildren.

The Frosts never had children of their own, so during their retirement years, they doted on the neighborhood children. As a young child, I don't recall asking them about their life before they came to Rockaway. I speculated that with their dental practice in Kansas City, they did not have time to devote to children. When they moved four hours south to the Ozark hills, we became their avocation.

The birthdays of the Beach children were special to the Frosts. Joan and I shared June birthdays, so we usually celebrated ours together. Dr. and Mrs. Frost arranged an outing to the Don and Jill Gardner Golf Ranch in Branson for my ninth birthday. Located six miles east of Branson, it was one of only two golf courses in the area. It had a driving range, clubhouse, restaurant, and eighteen-hole golf course. The Frosts took seven of us for an afternoon at the golf club, where they provided lunch and buckets of balls to hit from the driving range. They also provided exposure to something new and different for most of us.

The Gardners were from the Chicago area, and with her deep, husky voice, Jill had an artsy, creative, almost flamboyant air about her as she welcomed the little group of Rockaway children to the country club. That warm June afternoon when I turned nine years old, spent with two amazing couples, made me begin to realize that there was a sophisticated world out there that offered great possibilities beyond the little cocoon of my world in Rockaway Beach.

My friendship with the Frosts lasted until their deaths. After I had married and had my own children, they welcomed the second generation into their home with as much enthusiasm as they'd welcomed my siblings, my friends, and me. My children, Angela and Matt, were young when Dr. Frost died and Mrs. Frost left Rockaway to be close to her niece, but my memories are vivid of their delight in my children. The gift of time given to a child is a rare treasure; the gift of using one's time to enrich a child's life through unconditional love, acceptance, support, and encouragement was bestowed upon many children for more than two decades by this selfless couple.

The Paradigm Shift

The exodus started around noon, and by late afternoon, the Beach was empty. The packed crowds of only twenty-four hours earlier made their way back home on Labor Day afternoon, and the mom-and-pop business owners were giving a big sigh of relief, knowing they could have some much-needed rest with another busy summer season behind them. At this point, the moms and pops were assessing the success of the season, which was mostly limited to the months of April through August. It wasn't that fall or even year-round business had not been thought of; it had. It was a dream of the business owners, but in reality, most of the cottages were built in the thirties and forties with summer occupancy in mind, with screened in porches and minimum insulation. They weren't constructed to handle colder weather.

On Labor Day evening at our house, there was a complete paradigm shift. For five months, the focus was on the business. Mother and Daddy were on call around the clock. If guests arrived at midnight, one or the other had to greet them, show them to their cottage, and make sure their needs were met. We hired housekeepers only; Daddy did all of the maintenance, including lawn upkeep, repairs to the cottages, and supervision of our housekeepers. Mother handled all of the reservations, usually starting in February or March, via long-distance phone calls or US mail with our guests who came from many states. It was not unusual to have cars parked on our five to ten acres at the same time with license plates from

Illinois, Mississippi, Kansas, Louisiana, Texas, Tennessee, and the list goes on. They came year after year, always claiming their cottage.

Mother, who wrote by hand all of the correspondence regarding reservations in green ink on Michel's Cottage Court stationery with its green maple-leaf logo, knew in which cottage returning guests belonged when she heard from them each year. She devised her own method of maintaining records in an eleven-by-fourteen-inch ledger that she prepared each winter. The reservation book had each cottage number listed on its own page with a calendar handwritten individually for the months of the season. As the reservations came in, Mother circled, in pencil, the dates for each reservation; above the circled dates, she wrote the names of the guests for whom the cottage was reserved. It was amazing.

She kept meticulous records, and she taught Daddy, Francie, Sherry, and me how to take a reservation if she was not there when a phone call came in. It was a big responsibility to circle dates in Mother's absence. If we messed up and double-booked a cottage, or made a promise she couldn't keep, she had to straighten it out, and that didn't make her too happy, to say the least!

Oh, how a cell phone would have been appreciated by Daddy, because he was hands-on, always on the go, and unpredictable in where he might be found on the property. When a call came in, most callers expected to wait on the line while he was being located. It was challenging to find him, so as the number of cottages grew, he rigged up a bell system from the office that could be heard all over the resort. The bells were mounted on electric poles located in two or three spots around the property.

If he was needed to take a phone call or come to the office, we had codes. One ring meant "It's time to eat," because it was frustrating to have lunch or dinner ready for the family and not be able to find him. Two loud and long rings meant "We need you in the office *now* to take a call or talk to a guest." The guests, who also heard the ring codes, must have been impressed with such a sophisticated system of communication. I hadn't heard much about the word *technology* in the fifties or sixties, but I think Daddy got it!

We spent the summer months, day and night, catering to the needs and wants of our guests. We operated our resort before the days when it was popular to have a written mission statement, but if my parents had written one, I'm confident it would have been something like, "Our mission is to provide clean, comfortable accommodations and an enjoyable family-friendly vacation in a beautiful setting." Daddy and Mother strove to make our guests' stay as pleasant as possible. Along with our slogan "Follow the Leaves to Your Home in the Hills," the advertising also promised "Complete Housekeeping Cottages," and their goal was to make each cottage just that. Mother was particular about every detail; she paid attention to the curtains that covered the windows and the condition of the pots, pans, and utensils that filled the cupboards.

Daddy was convinced that being able to advertise a high-quality and comfortable bed would give us an edge in what was becoming a highly competitive market for the tourist dollar. He researched the quality of mattresses by visiting furniture stores in Springfield and Branson. After lying on many different brands himself to try them out and giving much consideration to the available choices, he determined that Simmons Beautyrest mattresses were the best quality, and all beds in the resort were changed to that brand.

Our highway signs soon had "Beautyrest Mattresses" added along with air-conditioning and TV and eventually free air-conditioning and TV by the late fifties when he decided to take the quarter meters off both. Comfort, cleanliness, aesthetics, and friendly service were the trademarks of our family business; these attributes were what attracted, as Mother used to boast, our share of the well-heeled guests who visited Rockaway Beach year after year.

One such family who visited the resort sadly left Rockaway Beach most likely vowing never to return. A lovely couple with their two boys, ages six and twelve, reserved one of the two-bedroom cottages for a week's stay. One day shortly after arriving, they had breakfast and lunch on the grounds, played in the pool during the day, and walked to the Beach in late afternoon to play Skee-ball, ride the bumper cars, or bowl in the open-air bowling alley.

As the afternoon turned into evening, they had dinner at Captain Bill's and headed back to the resort. Before starting their climb back up the hill, the family decided to stroll across the one-hundred-foot wooden-plank causeway that connected the shore on the town side of the Beach to the popular swimming island that was the hub of activity for lake swimmers and sunbathers during the busy summer months. The six-year-old, being rambunctious as boys can be, broke loose from his mother's hand, fell off the causeway, and plunged into the lake. Panicked and knowing that neither of his parents could swim, the older son jumped in to help his little brother. He was unable to reach the younger boy and unable to save himself. Both boys drowned.

It happened so quickly. Emergency units were called in, but it was too late. The devastated parents, barely able to move or breathe, were assisted back up the hill to the resort, and a long night lay ahead for Mother and Daddy as they tried to help them, comfort them, and make arrangements. During that long, mournful evening, law-enforcement people and a pastor were called in. All concerned did what they could to assist the young parents to contact relatives and begin their long grief-stricken journey and the journey of their sons, each in a black hearse, back to their home in Illinois.

Like a melting popsicle sliding from its stick on a hot summer day, the pressures of the summer season began to melt away during late afternoon on Labor Day. The next day was the beginning of fall in our world. It was the day that we started school, and it was the time of the year when we were not tourist-oriented. It was the season to do many things that we loved. As we returned home from the first day of school on Tuesday, the residents' collective sigh of relief was almost audible. The leaves on the trees seemed a deeper, more vibrant green; the sky seemed a brighter blue; and the air seemed a little more crisp than it had only twenty-four hours earlier. It was a new place, our little village, because it was only inhabited on this day by the locals. We loved our guests, but after Labor Day, we were a different kind of place, more private, more like other communities who participated in nontourist activities.

Francie, Sherry, and I, along with Joan, Karen, and other friends, were free to roam the Beach on our bikes and explore the woods, caves, or the little dam built by busy furry beavers native to our creeks and streams in the hills surrounding us. Even with a new school year beginning, we were free from the chores and responsibilities that came with being part of a family-owned business that depended on all family members to make it work.

The autumn and winter activities came along predictably the same every year. September was a time of winding down and settling into a schedule that included piano lessons, ballgames, cheerleading practice, and band trips. As the end of October approached, the Ladies' Club began planning the big Halloween event held upstairs at the schoolhouse, as it was always called, even when we no longer had school there. The upstairs was where Sunday school was held and all of the community events took place for the locals.

Halloween was a time for families to come together for an evening of fun, laughter, and an abundance of home-cooked food. There were prizes for the best costumes for adults and children, none of which were bought in a store. Some lucky children had mothers who sewed, but our mother didn't, so the girls and I had to get creative with what we could scrounge through in the attic or the storeroom. Among the most common of costumes for us were hobo, gypsy, or farm girl, with plenty of makeup, including bright red lipstick borrowed from Mother's makeup drawer or brown freckles drawn on our faces with her eyebrow pencil.

The adults' costumes were often the most ridiculous. They too were completely homegrown, and they were usually kept a secret from the kids. The routine was that they sent us to the party ahead of themselves and then walked in and surprised us with what they had put together. One of the most fun I ever remember was when Daddy put on an old dress of Mother's and came dressed as a woman, stockings rolled down to the ankle, pocketbook and all. By today's standards, that would be taboo, but it was hilarious for us girls to see our daddy, who always looked pretty spiffy, in such garb. We did not consider it strange but very comical. One year, Mother and Daddy came as Mr. and Mrs. Ghost, both simply covered in white sheets with holes cut out for their eyes, nose, and mouth.

A potluck meal was served, and then everyone bobbed for apples from a large water-filled galvanized tub placed on the floor. With no hands allowed, faces and hair got wet, but the first person in each round to pluck an apple from the tub by mouth got a prize. Was apple-bobbing sanitary? No. Was it fun? Yes.

After an hour or two of food and fun at the schoolhouse, everyone left and went home to receive trick-or-treaters. Groups of kids headed out and made the rounds to knock on doors and chant, "Trick or treat!" The folks of the Beach were wonderful hosts and greeted the youngsters with all kinds of homemade treats. They served caramel popcorn balls, homemade cupcakes, even ice cream cones along with chocolate bars, bubble gum, and all of the usual sugary treats. After a while, we headed home with our treasures, never entertaining the idea that future generations of children would not be allowed to accept homemade goodies from friends and neighbors as freely as we did in Rockaway Beach.

During the fall and winter months, we had Saturday-night dinners with our usual little group of three other families: the Puchtas, the Schneikarts, and Aunt Virginia and Uncle Lee. The four families were close neighbors and close friends and had years of shared experiences. There were fifteen of us in all, and eventually seventeen after Edwin and Rick Puchta, also a latecomer to his family, were born. Each family hosted a Saturday-night dinner once during the fall or winter, and what an occasion it was at our house! Mother was not easygoing when she entertained; she was a perfectionist.

First the housecleaning began. Every room had to be up to a

white-glove inspection. It didn't matter that these were our closest friends and family, and that they were in and out of our house on a regular basis. They knew that we lived in our house and it was not always in perfect condition. But from Mother's perspective, the Saturday-night dinner was held to a higher standard. She cleaned all week, and on Friday before the dinner, she cleaned the bathroom adjoining our bedroom, which was also the bathroom that our guests used.

When we got home from school on Friday afternoon, Francie, Sherry, and I each got a shoebox. In that shoebox, we were to put anything from our bathroom that we needed through Saturday night. That included toothbrush, toothpaste, deodorant, shampoo, curlers, or any of the other necessary commodities valued by teenage girls. We then traipsed down the long hallway toward Mother and Daddy's bathroom as if carrying out a military command. On a shelf emptied just for the occasion, we neatly lined our shoeboxes in a row, knowing we could not enter the forbidden territory of our own bathroom again until the Saturday night event had ended and our company had left the premises. Then we had permission to return to our confiscated space with its handsome built-in vanity Daddy had so diligently designed and constructed in our beautiful blue bathroom to house our stuff, and it once again became cluttered with our teenage paraphernalia.

On Saturday, the big day, the drill sergeant persistently present in Mother when the need arose emerged in full force, and we all got our marching orders. It was not a pleasant day! It began with removing all the good china from its place in the cabinets that were rarely opened. All the dinner plates, salad plates, and serving bowls had to be wiped with a clean towel just to be sure they were clean. Then the good silverware in the rectangular, blond-colored chest had to be retrieved and wiped clean, and the good glasses, likely purchased with S&H green stamps, had to be removed from their rarely abandoned spot in the cabinet, washed, and dried so that they sparkled and had no trace of a fingerprint that could be seen by the naked eye.

While we girls were doing these chores, Mother was doing the cooking. For the Saturday night dinners, the host and hostess prepared the meal; these were not potlucks, nor did the guests ask what they could bring. Our meals were not gourmet; on the contrary, they were simple but abundant. Mother's main course was usually ham, fried chicken, or some other type of chicken recipe. In addition to the main course, she prepared congealed salads, fresh salads, a relish plate, scalloped or mashed potatoes, vegetables, and dessert for this large crowd. Canned vegetables during winter months were the norm for our family, but for the Saturday-night dinners, Mother bought frozen vegetables. One of her favorites was frozen spinach, which was one of the first frozen vegetables we experienced during the fifties.

As the four families enjoyed food and fellowship on these fall and winter Saturday nights, bonds of love and friendship deepened. After the meal, parents and kids played games together, like charades or Uno, or in later years, had movie night when we viewed Kodak slides or home movies of good times we shared previously. The lives of our families were so intertwined that we knew no boundaries between good friends and family. Our friends were our family and our family members were friends.

During our teen years, we took the record player from its spot in the hallway outside our bedroom door to the office; closed the door so we wouldn't disturb the grown-ups; and did the jitterbug to songs of the fifties that we so dearly loved. We tried to teach Ken, who was Sherry's age, how to dance with us, but he wasn't interested. The little boys—Rick, Ed, and George Earl—just got in the way, but we tolerated them.

On Saturdays when we weren't hosting a dinner, we were much more relaxed. Every Saturday morning, Francie, Sherry, and I had our chores to do at home. We had to change our beds, clean our bedroom and bathroom, and dust and vacuum the living room and dining room. I felt very mistreated at the time because we had these chores. I used to long for a Saturday morning when this wasn't expected, but the only time that occurred was if we had school activities that interfered. We were motivated, however, on Saturdays to get up early and get our chores done so that we could go to town in the afternoon.

Before we left for Branson, usually around noon, we girls fixed Saturday lunch for the family, which was always the same menu: fried salmon cakes, fried potatoes, and buttered canned corn. After we had hurriedly rushed to get the dishes done, Mother or Daddy drove us to town. Our school friends met at Owen's Theater—the small theater on Commercial Street constructed from native fieldstone and boasting an authentic fireplace in the foyer—for the Saturday afternoon matinee. We watched the classics like *Giant, Gone with the Wind, The Lone Ranger,* and many John Wayne movies.

Francie usually met Bud Dunham there, her boyfriend since sixth or seventh grade, and her husband now of more than sixty years. I met my friends Jenny Caudill, Terry Akers, Wes Chase, and cousins Judy and Karen, and occasionally my friend David Whetstone. We sat together, bought popcorn and a Coke for a quarter, and then after the movie, went to Alexander Drug and had a double-scoop ice cream cone for a nickel. We saw some great movies at Owen's Theater.

The paradigm shift that occurred on Labor Day set the stage for the other part of my life. Summer months and days were full of wonderful experiences at the resort with guests, and in later teenage years, with summer jobs, but after Labor Day, I became a schoolkid, a playmate with my sisters and friends, and a basketball fan. I enjoyed life without too many responsibilities, except for Saturday morning housecleaning.

One of the most treasured experiences we had as teenagers was the planning of a late fall or Christmas dance. The five of us in our girl group chose a Saturday night for what we called a semiformal dance. Uncle Lee and Aunt Virginia allowed us to use the large dining room in Captain Bill's Hotel, and our mothers helped orchestrate a lovely, fun evening for our school friends. We created homemade invitations in the shape of a gold or autumn-colored leaf or a green Christmas tree. We dressed in our best clothes and party dresses and played our favorite records. We danced to the songs of Bobby Darin, the Platters, Elvis, and Ricky Nelson, among many of the fifties' top rock 'n' roll artists.

We served homemade fruit punch, homemade cookies, small sandwiches, and an assortment of chips and dips. All of our parents chaperoned and greeted our friends' parents as they dropped their children off and picked them up. We usually had fifty, sixty, or seventy teenagers in all of the high school grades attending our winter dance. It was always a huge success, and everyone had a great time. We were blessed that our parents were willing to devote their time and energy to us in such a special way.

Fall and winter in Rockaway were not boring. The Shrine Mosque in Springfield hosted the world-famous Shrine Circus almost every year. Captain Bill, a Shriner dedicated to the cause of helping young children who suffered from various health conditions, arranged for Beach children to attend the daylong Saturday event. Excitement mounted for weeks before the big day arrived. Early in the morning, accompanied by parents, we boarded the bus at the schoolhouse. Just as we were ready to depart for the winding and hilly trip along Old Highway 65 to the Shrine Mosque, Captain Bill climbed the two steps onto the school bus and wished us a great day. He then gave every child on the bus a ten-dollar roll of dimes to spend at the circus. A dime bought most concessions, and ten dollars bought a lot of circus trinkets!

Finally, we arrived at our destination on St. Louis Street in Springfield. The three rings inside the large hall were ceremoniously dominated by a tall, good-looking ringmaster decked out in black tie and tails. We were thrilled, entertained, and nervous as one daring act followed another, including elephants, lions, trapeze artists, and clowns,. Watching, from the edge of our seats, the elaborate and dashing acrobatic acts high above us, we assumed the mental role of great protector for each and every person who climbed the ropes toward the rooftop. As the acts became more and more daring, my concern escalated to the point that I wanted to scream to the performers, "You don't have to do this to entertain me! I want you to live!" Amazingly, no performers were ever injured while we were there. However, we had a close call on the Beach only a day or two after we returned from one trip to the circus.

Francie and Joan, about ten and eleven at the time, were greatly impressed by the tightrope walkers they had just seen, so they wanted to imitate them. There were two side-by-side trees, maybe fifteen feet apart, just outside the back door of our stone bungalow that we tied string onto and used for a clothesline for our doll clothes. It was three or four feet high, easily accessible to three little girls who wanted to take good care of their dolls. Scrounging around, Francie and Joan found a rope they thought suitable for their adventure and replaced the clothesline string with the larger rope a little higher up. They were proud of their achievement: the tightrope was ready, or so they thought. All they had to do was get across it from one tree to the other to claim boasting rights of acrobatic skills.

Francie admonished Joan, "You go first."

Joan, being the daredevil of the two and eager to go first, scooted up the tree onto the rope. After only a few perilous steps, she fell hard onto the rocky Ozark ground. She screamed in pain, and she and Francie both knew she was badly hurt. Parents were alerted, and Joan was rushed to visit Dr. Knowles, our local retired doctor who practiced medicine on the screened-in porch of his cottage half a block down the hill from us. He confirmed what Kenny suspected when he found Joan sprawled on the ground below the tightrope: her arm was broken. Fortunately, it healed, but once Mother and Daddy and Hazel and Kenny became aware of their girls' acrobatic aspirations, the amateur circus acts of Rockaway Beach abruptly ended.

The residents and business owners of the Beach worked tirelessly during the winter months to raise funds for the purpose of promoting tourism in our little village. Around Valentine's Day, pie suppers were popular, and a young suitor tried to buy the pie of the girl he wanted to sit with for the evening. Pies, wrapped in fancy packaging, often with large bows made from satin or crepe paper, were auctioned and sold to the highest bidder. The identity of the pie maker was kept a secret, but the bidding could get serious if a young man had his eye on someone special.

In Rockaway, the pie suppers were not only a good method of fundraising, they were a popular social event. The women, well known for their home-cooked food, prepared meals that drew residents from all across the region during the late winter and early spring months. With their assortment of meats, vegetables, salads, and desserts served upstairs in the schoolhouse, they gained a reputation as one of the best places in the area to get a good home-cooked meal for a reasonable price and for a good cause.

When the cottages began airing out in late March, Mother and Daddy allowed us, as teenagers, to host slumber parties with our school friends. Anywhere between ten or twelve girls would pack up what they needed for one night, and we would hang out from right after school on a Friday night until ten or eleven the next morning in a cottage large enough for us to have maybe a chair or a bed to sleep in—if we ever got around to sleeping. We had lots of good snacks, Dr. Pepper, and all-night conversations about boyfriends, teachers, and summer plans. Sixty years later, we still remember those special times with school friends.

The tourist season began to gear up once again in early April, when business owners recognized the need to work together for the good of the community. People were willing to help each other, volunteering their time and energy to get things done. Along Missouri Highway 160, there was only one way to drive into the Beach. Residents determined that the drive would be much prettier if some of that highway and especially the Y where tourists turned to get to the Beach were better maintained. It was the responsibility of the state but often ignored, so business owners, including Daddy and Kenny, took turns manicuring those spots to enhance the aesthetics of our area. They did their part to practice community service and realized how it positively impacted every business and resident on the Beach. As I recall, the simple act of Daddy and others taking the initiative and responsibility to maintain highway property that led to the Beach, I am reminded, once again, that lessons passed down to children and grandchildren are taught best by example, not words.

As seasons changed in the Ozark Mountains from autumn with its brilliant foliage in reds, oranges, and golds; to winter with its classic scene of a red bird perched on a bare branch; to the ever-faithful daffodil nodding its head in the March winds bringing with it the promise of spring, the people of Rockaway began preparing for a new season of summer. Warmer days of spring found proprietors raking leaves, painting the chipped wood of Adirondack furniture that would soon adorn well-watered green summer lawns, and tending to the colorful blossoms that would provide a plethora of color for the pleasure of our guests through the warm days of June, July, and August. And, as another season came to an end on another Labor Day, the great paradigm shift happened again for the families of Rockaway Beach. Within that ebb and flow, we were blessed with wonderful friendships, close family ties, and the bond of Christian brotherhood that cemented us together.

Thanksgiving Day

The fresh, plump twenty-five pound turkey was placed in its oval blue-and-white-speckled enamel roasting pan around midnight on Thanksgiving eve, long after we girls had gone to bed. Mother, being somewhat of a night owl, busied herself in the kitchen well into the night, preparing for the arrival of the Michel clan around eleven the next morning with their array of vegetables, salads, breads, and desserts to complement the turkey and dressing. When the aunts arrived, the bounty of homegrown and home-prepared foods was a testament to their gardening and culinary skills.

We enjoyed green beans grown in Auntie's garden and preserved for Thanksgiving Day through canning or freezing. We enjoyed Mother's carrot cake, applesauce cake, and apple cobbler, and Aunt Opal's pineapple upside-down cake prepared in a black cast iron skillet, glazed with caramelized brown sugar, turned upside down to release in its circular form, and topped with a bright red cherry. We counted on Aunt Jewell's pickled okra to bedeck the Thanksgiving spread, grown by Uncle Charlie in his garden and processed as only she knew how, with the right amount of garlic and vinegar dressing to make it tart but pleasingly sweet. A few pints were gifted to us by Aunt Jewell for Christmas each year, and because of Mother's praises and her stinginess to only open up a jar for the most special dinners of the year, we believed that we were experiencing a fine and rare food delicacy.

The fourth Thursday in November was a festive day as the

aunts, uncles, and cousins gathered to celebrate the holiday. When the cousins were little, it was chaotic, as any gathering is with small children, but as we grew and became young teens, we enjoyed the opportunity to be together. About twelve of us were stair-step in age, best friends, and schoolmates, so we eagerly anticipated the day and loved the camaraderie.

In addition to our first cousins, we looked forward to our second cousins, the Persinger boys, being with us. They were several years older than the first cousins. We admired them and loved the attention they bestowed on the younger set of cousins. They were athletic, and it made us feel important and privileged when we were in elementary and junior high to get the firsthand account of their high school and college activities. Gordon, attentive to all of us, shared what it was like to be a student at the University of Missouri, and he showed all nine of his younger girl cousins that we were special to him. He had an easy, homespun way about him that made us feel comfortable, but he also had an air of sophistication because he was older, wiser, and more experienced in worldly affairs than we who were still in elementary or junior high school.

When the feast was finished around one thirty or two in the afternoon, the cousins got creative and set out for other activities, depending on whose home we were in. In Rockaway, we divided up by age group and found things to do on our own. We often left the house and walked to the Beach, which had been devoid of tourists since the season ended after Labor Day. It was pleasant to have it to ourselves, and after age ten or eleven, we were allowed to explore without adult supervision.

Some of us loved taking walks along the causeway to the island, where we sat and drew pictures in the sand with a stick or ambled slowly through the woods behind the resort. Karen, Judy, Sharon, and I sat isolated in the woods on the banks of the small stream that trickled through the property behind the resort, undisturbed by anyone or anything, talking about boys, basketball games, and cheerleading, prompted by events around which our lives centered.

School, friends, church, family, and childhood dreams for the future comprised most of our conversations.

Another favorite place we explored was the small cave in the woods at the top of the big hill above our house. The opening was not large, but it was big enough to walk in ten or fifteen feet and be able to almost stand up. There was no entrance past the ten or fifteen feet, so it was another perfect hideout for adventurous little girls.

One year, when we were hosted by Aunt Virginia and Uncle Lee in their living quarters at Captain Bill's Hotel, we cranked up the record player, put on the latest Elvis hits, and danced the afternoon away in the large glassed-in porch with its hardwood floors and authentic wicker deco furniture overlooking the still waters of Lake Taneycomo. When Gordon and Glenn and cousin Ronnie were willing to dance with their younger cousins, we were thrilled and didn't want the day to end.

On Thanksgiving Day 1953, the Michel clan was hosted by Mother and Daddy. Mother had everything organized as usual in her characteristically efficient way. The multicolored Fiesta Ware dishes were taken from the cottages to add to what we used daily in the house so that there were enough matching plates for fifty family members or more. The plates were neatly stacked on the countertops, and the meal was served buffet-style. The kitchen table was set for eight, the dining room was set for ten, and card tables were set up in the large living room and the office so that everyone had a place to sit and eat. None of us, adult or child, was expected to juggle Thanksgiving dinner on our lap.

It was not unusual for us to prolong the day so that by late afternoon, we were ready to get out the leftovers and have another bite to eat before all the families headed home. Turkey and cornbread dressing were the mainstays of the meal and usually the first to be delved into for late-afternoon seconds. Thanksgiving Day 1953 was mild for an early winter day; so mild, in fact, that only some of the elderly folks donned coats. Mother and the aunts did not notice the mild temperature as they left the turkey and dressing sitting out all afternoon as usual. As family members began going back for another helping late in the day, it tasted even better than it had at noon, and that one last taste of turkey and dressing satisfied their need for food for the day as they began to think about another Thanksgiving coming to an end.

About midnight on that Thanksgiving Day, Mother, expecting our new baby brother or sister in April, became very ill. We girls heard the commotion that was taking place, and we didn't know what to think. Aroused from our sleep, we went into their room, and Daddy told us that Mother was very sick. As sick as she was, she got through the night, and the next morning, Daddy began talking to his brothers. He learned that several members of their families had suffered throughout the night with the same symptoms, and it was determined that the dressing being left out all afternoon had caused food poisoning.

Thankfully, Mother and all of the others recovered with no serious issues, but this was quite a learning experience for the Michel family. It was determined that if dressing has eggs in it, it should never be left at room temperature for more than an hour or so. After 1953, we became acutely aware of the risks of food poisoning, and Mother taught my sisters and me to be very careful with Thanksgiving dressing. Lesson learned: stash it away in the fridge as soon as dinner is over!

Thanksgiving Day with the Michel clan was always much anticipated. Our family traditions revolved around the attitude and teaching from our parents that we had much for which to be grateful. Among the blessings we enjoyed were love and appreciation for our large family and the opportunity to be together to celebrate the abundance bestowed upon us by our Creator. One of the last things we did on Thanksgiving Day was to draw names for Christmas. Names of all family members were put into a hat. Everybody drew one, and that was who we bought a Christmas gift for when we gathered again to celebrate Christmas with our loved ones.

Oh, Christmas Tree

Oh, the excitement of putting up the Christmas tree at our house! Sometime after mid-December, Mother, Hazel, and Aunt Virginia collaborated and announced the appointed day. Francie, Sherry, and I eagerly awaited the afternoon spent with Daddy, Uncle Lee, and Karen, along with Kenny, Joan, and little brother Ken, all of whom participated in the multifamily hunt for our Christmas trees.

When the agreed-upon day and time arrived, the three fathers dressed in warm pants, boots, and heavy gloves. They got out their sturdy handsaws, and nine of us hopped in the pickup truck. Six children also dressed in hats, mittens, colorful wool scarves, and long pants to protect us from the brisk December wind and cold sat on the floor of the pickup bed as we began our four- to five-mile trek to the Melton property on Highway F, where Hugh and Glessie Melton allowed us to wander through their densely wooded acres of bare-branched deciduous trees.

The woods were home to oaks, birch, walnuts, and an overabundance of species native to our Ozark hills, but it was the evergreen cedar that was the focus of our hunt, and we were very particular. With great gusto, we examined the prospects for the coveted tree of the year, looking at height, shape, and richness of the deep, dark green of which the tree could boast. Cedar trees are not known for their perfect form but can be rather lopsided.

Roaming tirelessly through the woods, we meditated on the needed approval of Mother. My sisters and I knew she had to like it, or back to the woods we'd go! Her look once it got plopped in the bucket with heavy rocks holding it up was the verdict. Will this one stay, or will we make a return trip?

The just-right tree—not too large, not too small, and not too lopsided after Daddy adjusted the trunk with his handsaw as many times as needed to meet Mother's approval—finally got propped up in the bucket. Plenty of water was poured into the bucket to keep the tree green and fragrant until the week between Christmas and New Year's, when it would have to come down because it was turning brown. The final touch was two or three white sheets draped around the bucket and onto the floor, in a fairly weak attempt to give the image of new-fallen snow.

After many years of propping the tree in a bucket, Daddy proudly brought home a red and green tree stand that actually had a place for water and could have water added to it as needed to prolong the life of the tree. This was one more example of Daddy's eagerness to embrace new and modern technology.

Prior to our trip to the woods, Daddy pulled down the built-in attic ladder in the garage and ascended its wobbly steps to retrieve the Christmas decorations, which were carefully placed in old-fashioned slatted and wooden bushel baskets that had originally been used for storing apples or peaches. Silver-flecked white felt carefully protected the colorful bubble lights and shiny ornaments each year when the decorations were put away, preserving them for many years. Rarely did we buy new lights or ornaments. There was a familiarity with each string of lights and each ornament that made decorating the tree a magical event.

The long arduous tasks of checking the bubble lights and colored bulbs tested my patience. Daddy had multiple strings of lights draped across the floor, plugged in together to try to find the faulty bulb that prevented all of the other lights from working. After what I perceived as hours, the lights were somehow working and strung on the tree. We then carefully unwrapped all of the glass ornaments and lovingly placed them on the tree so that it had ornaments all around it, front and back, up and down.

Then Mother brought out the newly purchased boxes of silver icicles. That was the one decoration she bought new each year, because they could not be easily removed when the tree was discarded. She insisted that each silver icicle had to be placed so that it was straight and even. It could not be thrown on the tree or land in a clump of silver.

The crowning touch of our glorious tree was the yellow neon star gently placed on the top branch, which Daddy had to do because he could reach it. Then all the old wooden storage baskets were put away, the floor was vacuumed to pick up the trail of needles from the live cedar tree, and everything in the living room was tidied and perfect for optimum enjoyment. At long last, it was time to revel in the magic of the season as the eyes of three little girls gazed into the reflection of the lights and ornaments, basked in the beauty and fragrance of our perfect Christmas tree, and experienced overwhelming feelings of safety, security, and excitement at home with our Mama and Daddy.

Post–World War II Christmas was a joyous time in Rockaway Beach. After Edwin was born, his big sisters found great delight in his delight in the Christmas season. As we gazed into the lights of our Christmas tree, we dreamed of what Santa might bring us.

It was not the custom in our home to make a list of what we wanted for Christmas, but we loved everything that appeared under the tree. Santa never wrapped his gifts. He usually left each of us a new doll, pajamas, robe, and house shoes. One Christmas that I remember was about my ninth. I tried on my new robe and was playing with my doll when Mother told Francie, Sherry, and me in a suspicious voice to keep looking, because Santa might have left something else.

After some serious hunting, we found, tucked among the wrapped gifts, three small, black-silk-lined faux-leather boxes. Our names were on the boxes, and when we opened them, to our great surprise and delight, we each found a simple gold watch with a narrow band and clasp. The resort must have had a banner season that year for us to have received such a special gift from Santa. It was my first grown-up gold watch. I would have never thought to ask for such a gift, but I proudly wore it on my left arm for many years to come as if it were of great worth.

Once we reached the age of ten or eleven, our final doll from Santa was a wedding doll adorned in wedding dress and veil. That was a lovely tradition that I passed on to my two daughters, Angela and Rebecca, who both received their own wedding dolls at the appropriate age. Traditions were ingrained into the fabric of life in our family and in our community. We thrived on them, and I learned at an early age that they brought peace and joy to our days.

Oh, Christmas tree, oh, Christmas tree, how lovely are your branches!

Christmas Eve

Beautifully wrapped presents were delivered to our friends on the Beach. Trays of home-baked cookies, candies, and breads were delivered to elderly friends whom Mother said might have no visitors for Christmas. Our final practice for the Christmas production had been completed. Butterflies fluttered in my tummy as I made my way up the narrow wooden staircase of the Sunday school building.

Christmas Eve, my favorite day of the year, had finally arrived, and the celebrations began to unfold. One of the most meaningful occurred on the unforgettable winter night of December 24. As children have done for generations, the children of the Beach were given parts in the reenactment of the nativity scene. The roles of Mary, Joseph, the wise men, and the angels were cast ahead of time, and the young actors practiced for the Christmas Eve service. Lights were turned down low in an attempt to mirror that glorious night in Bethlehem.

Mary was covered from head to toe in a piece of blue cloth, and Joseph was in a colorful draped cloth representative of that long-ago night. White sheets were converted to angel clothing, with wings and halos carefully crafted from cardboard, covered in white, and outlined in gold Christmas tree tinsel. The wise men donned bathrobes of royal red, blue, and purple. Rehearsals, directed by the Sunday school mothers, who had no training in theatrics but had hearts full of love for the birth of our Savior, resulted in productions that conveyed the Christmas message simply and beautifully.

Eight-year-old cousins—Judy, Karen, and I, in velvet Christmas dresses—sang a trio of "Silent Night" with heart and soul and fear, as if we were performing in Carnegie Hall. Kenny, ever the faithful service leader, praised the efforts of all the children and then led us in prayer. He spoke of the true meaning of Christmas, and the large room on the second floor of our one-room school rang out with the joyous sound of the old familiar Christmas carols.

As the service ended, we heard the faint tinkling sound of sleigh bells from a distance. They progressively became louder, and then we heard footsteps ascending the staircase. Suddenly, a surprise visit from Santa Claus added to the joy and wonder of the evening. Entering the room with a hearty "Ho, Ho, Ho!" he handed out apples, oranges, and candy in individual red net stockings to all present.

During the year, if our parents became aware of families in our community who were less fortunate, they helped us in organizing efforts to make those families' Christmas brighter. Among my fondest memories are of the times when we packed huge boxes of clothes and provided groceries for families who did not attend our Sunday school and never came to our Christmas service. We went to school with them. They were our neighbors.

When the Sunday school service ended around seven o'clock, we hurried off to our next celebration: the Michel family Christmas party, hosted by one of the eleven siblings. The whole clan gathered once again, as we so frequently did throughout the year. We feasted on an abundance of homemade delicacies, including ham, turkey and cornbread dressing, barbecued ribs, hot potato salad, gelatin salads, vegetables, and desserts galore. Each of the aunts could be counted on to bring what she knew was expected by members of the large extended family, and her name was automatically attached to the name of food, as if she had an international monopoly on it.

Aunt Jewell's homemade chicken and noodles was a favorite. Aunt Rose, born and raised in Germany and the war bride of Uncle Exie, introduced us to German cuisine with her authentic hot potato salad, and Aunt Virginia, though born in Taney County, made a German chocolate cake that was so tall I am convinced she must have doubled her recipe of batter and icing. Aunt Louise contributed her assortment of tens of dozens of cookies, cakes, and breads that she started making in October and froze for the holidays. She made pressed cookies shaped like miniature green trees, iced and glittering with holiday sprinkles; miniature poinsettias covered with white icing and red glitter; Waldorf Astoria (red-velvet) cake; and her signature Christmas pecan cake. Our elderly and slightly plump Cousin Ethel took delight in sampling each and every dessert spread before us; not large portions, but a dinner plate held a small piece of each homemade confection.

When the feasting subsided, it was time to enjoy our gift exchange. From the drawing on Thanksgiving Day, one name per person, everyone had one gift under the tree. Aunt Pearl, Daddy's youngest sister, received special attention because of her special needs. She got presents from everyone, and the cousins, all twenty-something of us who lived in Rockaway and Branson, loved pampering her. She entertained us with stories of her life growing up on the homestead with her mom, dad, and siblings.

Aunt Pearl had two special talents that greatly impressed me: she could recite the ABCs backwards, never missing or misplacing a letter of the alphabet, and she was able, when quizzed by name, to give the exact birthdate and year of each and every one of her nearly thirty nieces and nephews, never making a mistake. Christmas Eve was a special evening for Aunt Pearl. She relished the time spent with her family and loved the attention she received.

After the gift exchange, out came all of the Michel musical instruments, and the house was alive with toe-tapping music. Though unable to boast of a single music lesson among them, the siblings played guitar, fiddle, banjo, piano, and organ. Our homespun orchestra provided the perfect accompaniment for the singing of Christmas carols and the dancing of children in front of a warm fire. As the evening ran its course, the brothers and sisters told stories of growing up in these rugged Ozark hills and how they spent Christmas Eves with their own aunts and uncles and cousins in much the same way.

We were a large family who celebrated the birth of Jesus and proclaimed Him as our Savior; who prayed together before meals giving thanks for our abundance of blessings; and who knew how to have fun with each other. Christmas was indeed special in our big family, but the same genuine and loving concern for extended family manifested itself every day of the year. On many a dark December night when the family party ended and the siblings and their families headed to their own homes, the shining stars in the sky above reminded us of the bright star that shone two millennia ago, leading the wise men to Jesus. For a brief fleeting moment, we were blanketed in perfect peace on earth, thankful that the family members who came before us passed down the rich heritage that led us to the same Jesus and taught us to be confident that in Him, we have eternal hope.

Christmas Day

The anticipation of Santa sliding down the chimney into our living room on Christmas Eve permeated the night and created an aura of near magic in our household, if only for a few hours. When we arrived home from our Christmas Eve party with the Michel clan, Francie, Sherry, Ed, and I donned our PJs and gathered around the fireplace, with Ed on Daddy's lap as he read Clement Clarke Moore's *The Night Before Christmas*. The reading of that beloved Christmas story was nonnegotiable. We dreaded the final words of the poem, "Merry Christmas to all, and to all a good night," because we knew they signaled that it was time to go to bed and go to sleep, or Santa wouldn't find our house.

Expecting to hear the tinkling of sleigh bells and pounding of hooves on the roof, wondering what Santa might leave, and wondering what was in all those unwrapped presents under the tree, sleep came hard. But it came more easily that we wanted it to after a day and night of excitement. Finally, the first of us to awaken as the night slowly turned into morn alerted the other siblings, and after taking a sneak peek at what was under the tree and hoping we could convince them to let us stay up, we rushed into Mother and Daddy's room well before dawn and exclaimed, "Santa came! Santa came!"

Being roused from sleep that had not come hard to them and displaying surprise in their voices, suggesting that some small miracle had occurred, they responded, "He did?"

"Yes!" we shouted. "He did! He brought us dolls, and new

pajamas, robes, and house shoes." While we were asleep, these had just appeared under the tree, and they were in plain sight when we dashed out of bed and ran to the tree in the living room.

During Christmas week, usually on Christmas Eve, all four families in our group of friends who exchanged gifts visited the homes of the other families to leave their Christmas gifts, and they were under the tree to open on Christmas morning as well. After carefully examining our new dolls, what they wore, how their arms and legs moved, and what color their hair was, and after trying on our new robes and house shoes, we started unwrapping the gifts piled high around the base of the tree. Each gift was special, carefully chosen for its recipient, with beautiful wrapping destined to be torn in the wee early hours of Christmas Day.

The gifts were not expensive, but they were thoughtful. Sometimes for us girls, they were of a practical nature, like a box of Hallmark stationery. Sometimes they were of a more of a frivolous nature, like nail polish or a bottle of drugstore perfume.

Kenny was a little hard to buy for, but since he was known as a chocolate lover, Mother wrapped a one-pound box of Russell Stover chocolates for him every year, and every year, he told her and Daddy how much he loved getting such a great Christmas gift. He and Hazel also found Daddy a little challenging to buy for, so they, too, wrapped a one-pound box of Russell Stover chocolates and put it under the tree for him. It provided a good laugh for all of us when we talked about their decades-long exchange of Russell Stover chocolates on Christmas Day. Still today, I associate Russell Stover chocolates with the lifelong friendship we shared with Hazel and Kenny and their family.

Once the gifts had been opened early on Christmas morning, it was time to begin thinking about the trip to Brown Branch. Until I turned six years old, we went to Maplewood Farms in Brown Branch, the beautiful and spacious Victorian two-story childhood home of Mom Reese, where we gathered with Great-Grandpa Albert Dean. After Great-Grandfather Dean's death, we went to Mom and

Daddy Dow's for Christmas Day with the Reese family. Every year, it was the same routine. Mother put a big turkey in the oven around midnight on Christmas Eve. It cooked slowly all night long, and that familiar aroma greeted us at the crack of dawn, reminding us of the predictable routines of Christmases past and that we had another day of celebration and festivity ahead of us.

Christmas dinner was the same as Thanksgiving: turkey, cornbread dressing, and all the trimmings. The turkey, dressing, and giblet gravy were placed in containers and carefully packed into the trunk of the car for the forty-five-minute trip along the winding, hilly roads of eastern Taney County, along with presents for Mom and Daddy Dow and all the aunts, uncles, and cousins on Mother's side of the family. The aunts helped Mom Reese round out Christmas dinner with their assortment of vegetables, salads, and desserts.

Mother had four siblings, and they were all there with their spouses and children for Christmas Day. Our gathering with the Reese family totaled around twenty. The maternal cousins lived in other places, so we didn't get to see them as often as we would have liked, but we were close-knit. There were nine of us first cousins. The youngest one, Tommy, born with cerebral palsy, was wheelchair-bound throughout his brief life. We loved him dearly, talked to him, and tried to play with him when we got together, even though he was unable to talk or respond in any way. Until his death at age ten, he had to be fed like an infant, and I am inspired to this day by the love and patience shown to him by his parents, Aunt Elaine and Uncle Herb.

Uncle Herb was a tall man, well over six feet, and Tommy inherited his height. Throughout his young life, Tommy was tall and somewhat lanky, and the image of Uncle Herb cradling his nine-year-old son on his lap to feed him his Christmas dinner of mashed potatoes and other soft foods is forever engraved in my mind. He personified love through his gentle, tender affection toward the son he cherished so deeply.

Mom and Daddy Dow cut their Christmas tree from their own property and had it decorated before the family arrived. Entering their pretty Arkansas stone ranch-style home, with a blustering fire in the fireplace, multicolored bubble lights on their tree, and the table set for Christmas dinner, was a welcoming scene on a cold winter day. The reunion with our cousins Diana and Rosemary from Kansas City was what we most especially looked forward to, because we were close in age and loved playing together. The turkey, dressing, mashed potatoes, and Christmas salads were spread on the large kitchen table and as many as could gathered around. The remaining folks sat at card tables.

Mom did not have enough plates for everyone to have a dinner-sized plate, so the kids were given salad plates on which to eat our meal. I understood the reasoning for this, but I nevertheless always felt slighted. I have made it a point to offer my grandchildren a full-sized plate when we eat if they want one.

Mom had a big garden where she grew row after row of sweet corn. After harvesting, she spent countless hours preparing quart after quart of frozen creamed corn, and Christmas dinner was not complete without it.

After our noontime Christmas meal, the cousins wanted to go directly to the gift opening that we shared sitting around the fire with all of the family. Mom, however, was not in such a hurry. I have often thought that her main goal on Christmas Day was to test the patience of her young grandchildren and to provide them with a lesson on discipline and obedience while maintaining a cheerful heart and grateful attitude in the spirit of the true meaning of Christmas. Being the very cultured person and devout Christian that she was, she insisted that we read accounts of the Christmas story from the gospels of Matthew and Luke and then sing a nice selection of her favorite Christmas carols as she accompanied us on the piano. The cousins—Diana, Rosemary, Francie, Sherry, and I, along with the younger boys, Ed, Bill, and Alan—could hardly contain ourselves as we had to endure this long prelude to the gift-opening ceremony.

Finally, Mom yielded to the pleading, eager faces of her grandchildren and allowed us to get started on the most fun part of the day. Again, we experienced the opening of gifts with cherished loved ones, and again, they were not expensive gifts. They were, however, an expression of our deep love for each other and created memories that remain embedded in my mind of what a perfect Christmas Day should be. Going to Mom and Daddy Dow's home in Brown Branch was a tradition in our family that never was compromised, and I have no memory of spending Christmas Day anywhere else until I was married in 1965 and moved away from Taney County with my new military husband.

The holidays were a most wonderful time of year for us, with all of the family celebration and festivity. As I reflect back on the Christmas traditions of my childhood, gifts of great monetary value do not come to mind. In some cases, they were dime store finds, but it was the spirit with which they were given that has stayed with me all of my life. Mother and Daddy and the other adults on both sides of my family and among our close friends lived their lives demonstrating Christian values and morals, and that was the greatest gift they could have given us.

That gift was demonstrated in their lives every day of the year; it was not pulled out in November and December like special holiday linens for the table. Honoring traditions, making the time and effort to be with family, and keeping the focus on the birth of Jesus instilled in me a deep love and reverence for the holidays, which I treasured deep in my heart all the days of my life. Traditions help us know who we are and Whose we are and create a sense of security in a world riddled with uncertainty and difficulties. Traditions, centered on Jesus and family, during the Christmas season will create treasured lifelong memories.

Snow Days

Mother crept quietly into the dark bedroom where we lay snuggled among the quilted layers of our two side-by-side double beds and whispered quietly, "Go back to sleep, girls. School has been cancelled." The joy and excitement of a surprise snowstorm in the Ozarks was like getting an unexpected and treasured gift when we didn't have to go to school. Those words held magic, because a snow day in Rockaway Beach was a holiday for the whole community.

No one left the Beach because of the dangerous winding, hilly, and snow-packed roads. There were no snow-removal trucks or equipment in our little village. And no one cared! Some self-proclaimed expert drivers boasted that they could get anywhere they needed in an emergency by loading the back of their pickup with firewood. I heard that declared during every snowstorm, but I have no recollection of that kind of emergency occurring.

During the winter months, Daddy worked with Uncle in his construction business to supplement our seasonal resort business income, but he stayed home on snow days, and because most of our neighbors were business owners who did not commute to other jobs, children and adults alike were out and about on foot traversing our snow-packed hills by mid-morning. Our mentality was, "This is going to be a fun day; no work, no school, no homework, no practicing the piano, no chores." We understood that it was a day to play.

When we girls finally rolled out of bed, we were greeted by the glowing red, orange, and blue embers of a brand-new fire. We peered out the window at the snow-covered landscape in awe and wonder, relishing its beauty as if it were a playground created for our personal pleasure and enjoyment. Daddy fixed flapjacks for breakfast, and before long the landlines (all we had) started ringing. Joan, Ken, and Karen wanted to know when we were planning to come out. Mother and Daddy encouraged us to get outside, but we were admonished to bundle up because it was cold.

Bundling up in the 1950s meant putting on two undershirts, two pairs of heavy socks, a couple pairs of our warmest pants, and more than one heavy sweater. Next came a heavy coat, mittens, a stocking cap or wool scarf tied under our chin, and finally those awful black rubber galoshes that made moving about more an exercise in clomping than walking. It was cumbersome, to say the least, and a huge inconvenience to go in and shed it all momentarily if nature called. The styles and fabrics were not as streamlined as twenty-first-century attire, and once they got wet, they stayed wet the rest of the day, but the fun to be had was worth that sacrifice.

Daddy dressed for outside as well, and he trekked down to the cavernlike basement of our old bungalow where he kept our American Flyer sled with its base of three wooden slats sporting red side bars, blades, and a steering wheel. Our snow-covered hills were perfect for sledding, and we were accustomed to walking up and down them, which made it easy to take turns. Two or three of us sledded down the hill while the rest of the group waited at the top. After the exhilarating ride down, we walked back up dragging our sleds behind us to give someone else a much-awaited turn.

After a few hours of freezing in our soggy, wet clothes, we went home, changed into dry clothes, and decided to stay inside. As we sat in front of a warm fire, how scrumptious was homemade hot chocolate! There was no instant hot chocolate from a box, so Mother made it from scratch using the recipe on the side of the familiar dark brown Hershey's Cocoa can with its pop-up metal lid. Beginning with water, the ingredients were mixed, stirred, sweetened, and brought to a boil before the milk was added. Heated ever so slightly once the milk was added, it was carefully poured into individual mugs and then topped with a dollop of fresh whipped cream.

As the afternoon wore on, we often set up card tables and struck up a game of Monopoly, Uno, or dominoes (about the only games we ever played) with our friends and sometimes our parents. Almost without exception on snowy days, Mother started a batch of chili in her big, oval, hammered aluminum pan with the black-knobbed lid and let it simmer all afternoon. At day's end, with our family sitting around the yellow Formica table in the kitchen, we enjoyed hot chili and crackers and lots of boasting among the sisters about who was the best at sledding up and down the hills. The day ended with us wondering how far the thermometer would dip during the night and whether announcer Gene Gideon on radio station KBHM would grace the airwaves the next morning with the same welcome news that school would be closed again.

1962–1965 and Beyond

New Flint Hill School was not under the jurisdiction of any state regulation, as far as I know, so when Mother and Daddy explored the idea of enrolling me at the age of five years and three months as a first-grader, they determined that it would be in my best interest. Without exception, I was always the youngest person in my class, but it didn't present any particular challenges. I held my own with my classmates and graduated from Branson High School in May of 1962.

That fall, I started my freshman year at Southwest Missouri State College in Springfield at barely seventeen years old. My young age compared to other students in the freshman class of SMS suddenly was a negative. I felt completely out of place. I struggled socially and did not have an enjoyable first year of college. I felt awkward in most social situations and lacked confidence in myself.

During the late summer months of 1962, when the good-looking young Airman David Whetstone—dressed in Bermuda shorts and madras shirt, with his crop of well-groomed dark black hair shaved military style—arrived on campus to visit me, we approached our friendship from a new perspective. We felt a bit more grown up, as we were entering new chapters in our lives. He was stationed by this time in Cheyenne, Wyoming, at Frances E. Warren Air Force Base, and I was navigating the uncertain waters of college life.

Several weeks after he left Springfield, on the evening of October 23, I was notified by the RA in my dorm that I had a long-distance call in the booth that served as the community phone on our floor. David surprised me with a phone call occasionally, so I rushed to the phone. He greeted me in his sweet voice and asked how I was doing. I sensed that something special was taking place in our relationship and that he was growing increasingly important to me. I heard an unfamiliar strain in his voice that made me a little uneasy, and my head was swirling with curiosity.

I was about to be jolted as I had never been in my short life of seventeen years. He gave me the very somber news that F. E. Warren Base was on high alert. I was alarmed by the sound of it but had no idea what that meant. David explained that Nikita Khrushchev of Russia wanted to place nuclear missiles in Cuba, ninety miles from Florida. He further explained that the United States had established a naval blockade to prevent the missiles from reaching Cuba, and the US and Russia were in a military showdown. It was alarming!

With his training in intercontinental ballistic missiles, his military duties positioned David at missile sites across the state of Wyoming and in neighboring states almost every day. He clearly understood that the threat of nuclear war with Russia was a very real possibility, and that's what he told me that night of October 23. I felt frightened by the imminent threat of war in our country and by the idea that he could be directly involved in it because of his active duty. I grew up a little bit that night as I squeezed myself into the tiny phone booth in the hallway of my dorm, realizing that the possibility of nuclear war could affect this man who was becoming very dear to me. Thankfully, through God's mercy and the leadership of President John F. Kennedy, nuclear war was averted, and after thirteen tense days, an agreement was reached, the crisis ended, and David assured me that he was safe.

Safe, but separated by eight hundred miles, we bemoaned loneliness for the other in our constant stream of letters and occasional phone calls. We wanted to spend more time together, and by the time the academic year ended in the spring of '63, David and I had decided that we probably wanted to spend the rest of our lives together. Our ages—by that time eighteen and twenty years old—didn't concern either of us. Many friends, and even Francie and her childhood boyfriend, Bud Dunham, were married. It was a different time, and the custom was to marry young.

I was, however, committed to finishing college because my dream was to become a theater teacher. I began thinking about how I could possibly be close to David and still be able to continue my education. I believed that my struggles at SMS were because I was not able to see him but a few times a year, and I believed that I was missing what should be one of the best times of my life—an opportunity to be with one person in the world who had captured most of my thoughts and had become the central figure in my dreams for the future.

Cross-country travel by passenger train was popular in the early sixties, and I had no qualms about traveling alone. Mother and Daddy, on the other hand, had plenty of reservations about my adventurous spirit. But at eighteen, I was confident in my own ability to make arrangements and travel without adult supervision, so with money I had saved from summer work, I made plans to visit David in Cheyenne. I took a Greyhound bus from Springfield to Kansas City. I left Springfield late in the evening, and my bus would arrive in Kansas City at one or two in the morning. Not wanting to be out alone at that hour, I contacted one of Mother's sisters, Aunt Mildred, and her husband, Uncle Vernon, who lived there, and asked them if they would meet me at the bus station.

Without any hesitation, Uncle Vernon agreed to meet me, even in the middle of the night. What a saint he was, because he had to get up early for his job. I appreciated his effort and thanked him. This kindness shown to me by Uncle Vernon during those years when I made trips back and forth to Wyoming and Colorado created a unique and special bond with him that I might never have had. With time and age, I am even more thankful for his amazing generosity toward me.

He met me at the Greyhound bus terminal and drove me to what has been declared one of the greatest railroad stations of the early twentieth century, Union Station. He parked, walked me in, got me to my boarding area, and then returned home for a short night's sleep before going to work the next morning. I am so thankful he was willing to meet me and take care of me, because in my eagerness to make such a trip, I didn't consider all that could have happened to a young girl traveling alone in the dark of night.

Union Station was large and spacious, with grand high ceilings and comfortable waiting rooms. Cross-country railroad patrons dressed in their best attire to travel, expecting to dine in the white-tablecloth dining car at some point during the journey. I was able to buy a ticket straight through from Kansas City to Denver, a twenty-four-hour ride. Once I bought a ticket with a berth, but I decided that it was too much trouble to do that for only one night and chose to sleep in my seat on the one or two future trips I made by the same mode of transportation.

I did, however, enjoy going into the dining car for dinner or breakfast and had no insecurities about dining alone. Dining guests were served by waiters in hip-length white serving jackets, and tables were elegantly set with fine china and silver serving utensils. It was a pleasant way to spend time on a long journey.

If he could arrange it, David picked me up in Denver and drove us to Cheyenne, where I stayed with a lovely family who had befriended him as a young airman. If he could not get leave from the base, I would make another connection in Denver to the Greyhound bus and travel the last leg of the trip by bus to Cheyenne.

Directly south of Cheyenne about fifty miles was the pretty little college town of Greeley, Colorado. While coniferous and evergreen trees dotted the campus of Colorado State College and exuded beauty, the offensive and pungent smell of the stockyards was always present. The barnyard smell, however, was not enough to discourage me from being enamored with the school and the town, and I began looking into the idea of transferring there for my second year of college.

Although my interest in the college was based solely on its proximity to Cheyenne, I was pleasantly surprised to learn that the school had a strong education program and theater department with its Little Theater of the Rockies. David and I thought it would give our blooming relationship an opportunity to develop if it was meant to be. When presented with the idea, however, Mother and Daddy were not so keen on it. My travels to the West alone had made them both nervous. They were supportive because they trusted me and they thought highly of David, but to send me so far away from home for an extended period of time was not an idea they relished.

After I applied to Colorado State College in the spring of 1963 and was accepted, and after much prayer and convincing from me, they finally agreed. In late August of 1963, David went to visit his family in Alabama and then came to Rockaway Beach. My bags were packed for the next school year, and David's two-door '59 tan Chevy Bel-Air was loaded with skirts, sweaters, boots, coats, and scarves as we set out for Greeley. As we were about to drive off, Daddy handed David a twenty-dollar bill and said, "David, this is for Marilyn to have her own room when you stop tonight."

David replied, "Thanks, Vernie. She will have her own room, and I'll take good care of her."

I stayed in Webking Hall on campus, took a full load of classes that fall, and delved into activities involved with theater. I loved it, and David came to Greeley most weekends. For the first time in our courting days, we got to spend time together. We took long walks, enjoyed picnics, and talked for hours on end. We went to movies and dances, and he supported me in my endeavors with the Little Theater of the Rockies. His support meant a lot to me, because no family members were there for performances. The academic year at Colorado State was divided into four academic quarters. During the third quarter, I had some minor health issues that required attention, and I had to leave in March. I did not return.

Not quite a junior, the following fall, I entered the University of Missouri. In a long-distance relationship once again, David and

I decided that we needed to take a break and date other people. I enjoyed university life, once again getting involved in theater classes, attending football games, and making new friends. I started seeing one young man and dated him during the first semester.

In October of 1964, David drove through Missouri after visiting his family in Alabama and stopped in Rockaway to visit my parents. He was not sure if he wanted to or if I wanted him to stop in Columbia to see me, but after a long conversation with Mother and Daddy, he decided that he would. I enjoyed seeing him, but as the evening ended, we decided that our relationship was not to be. We bid each other a warm and sincere farewell, he headed for Cheyenne, and with a heavy heart for all we had shared through the years, I returned to my dorm room with the salty taste of tears flowing down my cheeks and onto my lips.

For several weeks, a dark cloud hung over me. I had difficulty focusing on my classes, and my grades plummeted. I found no solace in the company of the young man I had been dating. I thought I wanted the freedom to date others without any feelings of guilt, but once I gained that freedom, it lost its appeal. The satisfaction of my theater involvement lost its appeal as well; it became a burden. I didn't know what had overtaken me, but something unidentifiable had. Of that, I was sure!

As the semester was winding down, I looked forward to the holidays at home with the family. All I wanted to do was just go home. On a Sunday afternoon in December, 1964, trying to cram for final exams, I got a phone call from David—the only one we'd had since he left Columbia for Cheyenne in October. A little surprised that he called, I was guarded. After a brief exchange of trivial conversation, he said, "Marilyn, I am missing you, and I'm going to ask you something. Will you marry me?"

Like being immersed in cool water from a natural flowing stream on a hot day, I felt relief overwhelm me. I knew instantly what had been wrong with me during the course of the last weeks. I knew then that he was the one person in the world with whom I wanted to share the rest of my life. As I stood in the rays of the warm sun beaming through the plate-glass windows of my fifth-floor dorm room on that winter afternoon, his words were a soothing balm to my broken spirit. I said, "Yes, David, I will marry you."

During the second semester, I did not return to the University of Missouri. My education was put on hold while I stayed in Rockaway, and with Mother, always my advisor and best friend, planned my wedding. On March 14, 1965, when we were nineteen and twenty-one, David and I were married. Fifty-five years later, with three children and seven grandchildren, I can say that we have lived a richly blessed life.

We have had our share of difficulties, but through a deep faith in God that was introduced to us at a very young age and flourished in both of our childhood homes, we have survived challenges and thrived. Our parenting and grandparenting aspirations have been centered around our desire to teach the same values with which we were nurtured, and my deep conviction is that because of that, our children and their children have brought us much joy through the years. As I navigate through the senior years of my life, I have come to the conclusion that there are only three things needed to live a successful life: faith in God and obedience to Him, the love of family and friends, and, of course, good food!

Postlude

Recalling these stories makes me realize how blessed I was to grow up in Rockaway Beach. Reflecting on them actually makes me question whether some people will believe that they are true. One point I want to make is that we were not a family that was problem-free. Quite the opposite. We had many challenges during my growing up years; we had events that brought us sorrow, like the death of baby brother Michael Reese, and we had significant and permanent loss of business and financial setbacks after the proclaimed riot in 1965. Furthermore, Daddy suffered from bouts of depression off and on before medication was available to treat it, and he died of cancer at the young age of fifty-seven, leaving Mother a widow at forty-nine with a business to run and thirteen-year-old Edwin to raise alone.

I find joy in the fact that the good memories far outweigh all others. We are products of our upbringing, and people often tend to parent as they were parented. Mother and Daddy had a balanced approach to raising children. They taught me the value of hard work, and they let me know that they were appreciative of my contribution to the family business efforts even at a young age. They gave generously to my siblings and me of their time and attention. They were involved in every activity that was important to us. Most importantly, they took us to Sunday school and church. They did not drop us off and pick us up when the service ended.

Sixty to seventy years after most of these events occurred, I see a much different world. I am saddened by the breakdown in families, fatherless homes, and homes where the Bible and Christian values are not being taught. I am deeply convinced that if parents provide their children with the spiritual nourishment they need, many of the problems facing our society will diminish. Responsibility, kindness, and compassion are only a few of the character traits that we see slipping away from our culture. They start at home. When children see positive character traits modeled, they learn from them and copy those actions. Parental influence is greater than any other influence on earth. My prayer is that children everywhere will see Christ-like behavior in parents, grandparents, friends, and the larger community, and desire to emulate the behavior they see.

Our home and resort

The gateway to fun for "kids of all ages

Easter Sunrise on the shores of Lake Taneycomo

The Michel brothers and their wives. Aunt Pearl, first row on the left and cousins Ruby and Ethel Persinger beside her

*Mother's Day, 1950. Left to right, Sherry, Mother, me,
Daddy (with a white rose on his lapel), and Francie.*

An afternoon swim at Bull Creek

Daddy and I on a cool Easter morning, 1954

Francie with her Big Chief tablet on the first day of school

Louise Reese celebrating graduation from Southwest
Missouri State Teacher's College, 1939

Newlyweds Vernie and Louise Michel, 1940

The popular Lake Queen cruising from Rockaway Beach to Branson

4th of July crowds on the Beach

Summer attractions on the Beach included water sports,
shopping, and strolling the lakeside shops

The swimming island was the big draw for paddle
boards, and non-motorized paddle boats

Hotel Rockaway (also called The White Hotel)

The sun porch of Captain Bill's Hotel where guests enjoyed the soft, gentle afternoon breeze during summer visits, and where the cousins danced the day away on Thanksgiving afternoon.

Miss Casey and grades one through eight. I'm second row, second from the left. Francie is third row, second from left. Joan is third row, third from left, and Karen is third row, fifth from the left.

My sister-in-law, Vickie sitting on a wagon spring seat in front of one of the cottages. Repurposed for unique lawn furniture, they were repurposed even further to provide transportation in the back of the pick-up for the mamas and the kids when we went to the creek.

All grown up and married, I still loved to drop in and visit with Dr. And Mrs. Frost.

David and I with our children and grandchildren at the log cabin on the Michel Homestead where the twelve children of Ed and Rebecca Michel were born and raised with no electricity and no running water.

Our official 50th Wedding Anniversary photo, 2015

Cookbook of
Family Recipes

The social events of our family and friends revolved around good food, and my story would not be complete without including the generations-old recipes we treasure. On the following pages are recipes that have been enjoyed and passed down in our family for more than a hundred years, and they provide a backdrop to the stories I share. From Grandma Michel's basic Light Bread recipe, requiring sixteen cups of flour to make a batch large enough to sustain her family of thirteen on the Homestead, to the abundance of breads, Christmas cookies, and cakes that Mother served for decades at her elegant Christmas teas, food as a powerful force that brought friends and loved ones together, provided opportunities for rich fellowship, and created memories and stories that lasted a lifetime.

"Happy eating" from the recipes of the Michel and Reese women and the women of Rockaway Beach, our home in the hills.

Breads and Rolls

Mother's Snow Biscuits

Makes 10 to 12 biscuits.
1 package yeast
2 cups flour
1 tablespoon shortening
1 teaspoon salt
1 1/2 teaspoons sugar

1. Preheat oven to 400 degrees F. Grease an 8-by-11-inch pan.
2. In a small bowl, dissolve yeast in 1 cup warm water.
3. Add flour to a large mixing bowl. Cut shortening into flour with a fork. Add salt and sugar, and mix well. Stir in yeast.
4. Roll out dough on a floured board. Form biscuits with a biscuit cutter. Place biscuits on prepared pan. Let rise for about 1 hour.
5. Bake biscuits for about 15 minutes.

Grandpa Vernie's Flapjacks

Makes 5 to 8 pancakes.
2 cups flour
4 teaspoons baking powder
2 teaspoons sugar
1 teaspoon salt
2 eggs, beaten
2 cups whole milk
2 tablespoons liquid shortening

1. Sift all dry ingredients into a large bowl.

2. Add milk, beaten eggs, and liquid shortening, and beat with a whisk until smooth. A few lumps left in the batter is okay.
3. Heat a grill or skillet to about 400 degrees F and oil slightly. Pour on 1/2 cup batter to make a 4-inch-diameter pancake. Let one side fill up completely with bubbles, then turn to other side and cook until golden brown. Once flipped, cooking time will be shorter than on the first side. Repeat with remaining batter. Depending on the size of your skillet or grill, you may cook multiple pancakes at a time.

Tip: Diameter size of pancake can be adjusted to your liking by adjusting cup size portion.

Best-Ever Corn Muffins

Makes 8 muffins
1 cup cornmeal
1 cup boiling water
1/2 teaspoon salt
1/2 cup cold milk
1 egg, beaten
2 teaspoons baking powder
1 teaspoon melted butter

1. Preheat oven to 475 degrees F. Grease muffin pans.
2. Add cornmeal to a large bowl and pour boiling water over.
3. Add salt, cold milk, beaten egg, baking powder, and lastly, melted butter. Stir until all ingredients are blended.
4. Pour batter into prepared pans and bake for 25 minutes.

Mother's Waffles

Makes 6 (6-inch) waffles
4 eggs, separated

3 cups flour
4 teaspoons baking powder
1/2 teaspoon salt
2 cups milk
1/2 cup melted butter

1. In a large bowl, beat egg yolks well. In a medium bowl, stiffly beat egg whites.
2. In a separate large bowl, sift dry ingredients together.
3. Add sifted dry ingredients and milk alternately to egg yolks. Then add melted butter and fold in egg whites.
4. Add batter to a waffle iron and cook according to manufacturer's instructions.

South-of-the-Border Corn Bread

Makes 8 (5- to 6-ounce) slices
1 teaspoon cooking oil (for coating the skillet)
1 1/2 cups cornmeal
1 1/2 cups creamed corn
1 cup milk
2 tablespoons chopped hot peppers or red peppers (optional)
2 tablespoons chopped green onion
2 tablespoons chopped sweet green pepper
1 tablespoon baking powder
1 tablespoon sugar
1 teaspoon salt
1/2 cup canola oil
1 cup shredded cheddar cheese, or cheese of your choice (for topping)

1. Preheat oven to 450 degrees F. Coat a 10-inch cast iron skillet with cooking oil and heat in oven until hot.
2. In a large bowl, combine all ingredients except for shredded cheese and mix well.

3. Remove heated skillet from oven. Pour in batter and top with shredded cheese. Bake for 30 minutes. Cut in pie shaped pieces to serve.

Lemon Poppyseed Bread

Makes 2 loaves

Bread:

3 cups minus 2 tablespoons flour
2 1/3 cups sugar
3 eggs
1 1/2 cups milk
1 1/8 cups vegetable oil
1 1/2 tablespoons vanilla extract
1 1/2 tablespoons almond extract
1 1/2 tablespoons butter-flavor extract
2 tablespoons poppy seeds

Glaze:

3/4 cup sugar
1/4 cup lemon juice
1/2 teaspoon vanilla extract
1/2 teaspoon almond extract
1/2 teaspoon butter flavor extract

1. Preheat oven to 350 degrees F. Grease and flour two 8 1/2-by-4-inch loaf pans.

Make bread:

2. In a large bowl, mix together flour and sugar.

3. In a medium bowl, beat eggs and combine with milk. Add to dry ingredients.
4. Add vegetable oil; vanilla, almond, and butter extracts; and poppy seeds. Mix well with an electric beater.
5. Pour batter into prepared pans and bake 70 minutes.
6. *Make glaze:* In a small bowl, combine all ingredients. Pour over loaves while they are still warm.

Aunt Virginia's California Coffee Ring

Makes 10 to 12 servings

Cake:

2 sticks butter or margarine
1 cup sugar
3 eggs
1/2 cup whole milk
1/2 cup condensed milk
1 teaspoon vanilla
3 cups flour
1 teaspoon baking powder
1 teaspoon salt

Topping:

1/2 cup sugar
1/2 cup chopped pecans
3 teaspoon cinnamon

Glaze:

1 cup powdered sugar
1/2 teaspoon vanilla

3 tablespoons milk

Garnish:

10 to 12 whole pecans

1. Preheat oven to 350 degrees F. Grease and flour a 10-inch Bundt pan.
2. *Make cake batter:* In a large bowl, cream butter or margarine with sugar. Add eggs, whole milk, condensed milk, and vanilla. Sift together flour, baking powder, and salt. Add to batter and blend with an electric mixer.
3. *Make topping:* In a large bowl, combine all ingredients.
4. *Assemble cake:* Pour half the cake batter into prepared pan. Sprinkle topping on first half of batter. Add remaining batter and then remaining topping. Bake for 45 minutes.
5. *Make glaze:* In a small bowl, combine ingredients and beat well.
6. *Finish cake*: Pour glaze over coffee cake while it is still warm. Arrange whole pecans on top.

Mrs. Willis's Cranberry Orange Bread

Mr. and Mrs. Willis retired to Rockaway Beach from Chicago and opened a high-end gift shop. It did not include the usual Ozark-type souvenirs depicting the hillbilly images that were prevalent in those days. Their selection of merchandise included fine English bone china and beautiful French Limoges pieces. On Mother's Day, Daddy would give Francie, Sherry, and me a ten-dollar bill to choose a gift for Mother. Some of my most treasured keepsakes came from the Willis Gift Shop.

Makes 1 loaf
2 cups sifted flour
1 cup sugar

1 1/2 teaspoons baking powder
1/2 teaspoon baking soda
1/2 teaspoon salt
1 egg, beaten slightly
2 tablespoons melted butter
1/2 cup orange juice
2 tablespoons hot water
1/2 cup nuts
1 cup coarsely cut cranberries
grated rind of 1 orange

1. Preheat oven to 350 degrees F. Grease a 9-by-5-inch loaf pan.
2. In a large bowl, sift together dry ingredients. Add egg, melted butter, orange juice, and water; mix only until dry ingredients are moistened. Fold in nuts, cranberries, and orange rind.
3. Pour batter into prepared pan. Let stand 20 minutes, then bake for 50 minutes or until done.
4. When cool, wrap in waxed paper and store in bread box. Bread improves in flavor and slices more easily if allowed to stand 24 hours before cutting.

Buttermilk Coffee Cake

Makes 10 to 12 servings

Cake:

1 pound brown sugar
2 sticks butter
3 cups sifted flour
1 teaspoon baking soda
1/8 teaspoon salt
1 cup buttermilk
1 egg

Topping:

1 cup chopped nuts
1/2 cup sugar
1 teaspoon cinnamon
1 cup reserved cake mixture

1. Preheat oven to 325 degrees F. Grease a 9-by-13-inch pan.
2. *Make cake:* In a large bowl, blend together sugar, butter, flour, soda, and salt. Reserve 1 cup of this mixture for topping. Add buttermilk and egg to remaining mixture in bowl. Blend well, but do not beat. Spoon into prepared pan.
3. *Make topping:* In a small bowl, combine nuts, sugar, and cinnamon with reserved mixture. Sprinkle over cake batter in pan and press into batter with a spoon.
4. Bake for 30 to 35 minutes.

Hazel's Sour Cream Coffee Cake

Makes 8 to 12 servings

Topping:

1 cup chopped nuts
1/3 cup brown sugar
1/4 cup sugar
1 teaspoon cinnamon

Cake:

1 cup sugar
1 stick butter
2 eggs
1 teaspoon vanilla

1 cup sour cream
2 cups flour
1 teaspoon soda
1 teaspoon baking powder
1/2 teaspoon salt

1. Preheat oven to 325 degrees F. Greased a 9-by-13-inch pan.
2. *Make topping:* In a small bowl, mix together all ingredients.
3. *Make cake:* In a large bowl, cream together sugar and butter. Add eggs, vanilla, and sour cream, and mix well with a beater. In a separate bowl, sift together flour, soda, baking powder, and salt. Add to wet ingredients and blend all together with a mixer.
4. Spread half the batter in prepared pan; sprinkle on half the topping. Spread rest of batter on top and then rest of topping. Bake for 30 to 40 minutes.

Grandma Michel's Light Bread

This recipe is from the early twentieth century. I always heard Daddy talk about the light bread his mother made, and this is her recipe. It does not include directions, oven temperature, or length of time to bake. The 14 to 16 cups of flour undoubtedly makes a large amount of bread, as needed for feeding the large Michel family. Since this recipe was originally cooked in a wood stove, I recommend looking at other bread recipes for suggested oven temperatures and baking time.

4 cups scalded milk
3 tablespoons shortening
2 tablespoons sugar
4 teaspoons salt
1 cake yeast (comparable to a 1/4-ounce package of dry yeast), dissolved in 1/2 cup lukewarm water
14 to 16 cups flour

1. In a mixing bowl, combine scalded milk, shortening, sugar, and salt. Cool to lukewarm and add yeast dissolved in water.
2. Stir flour in gradually, mixing to a stiff dough that will not stick to hands or bowl. Knead lightly on floured board until dough is smooth and elastic to touch, about 10 minutes.
3. Place dough in a greased bowl closely covered and let rise in a warm place (82 degrees) until double in bulk. Knead lightly about 2 minutes and let rise again. Place in five to six greased loaf pans. Internal temperature should reach 200 degrees F.

Comfort Foods: Meat and Casseroles

(Just What the Doctor Ordered)

Southern Fried Chicken

The ingredient amounts can be adjusted for more or less chicken.
Serves 4 to 8
3 eggs
2 cups whole milk
3 cups flour
3 to 4 cups solid all-vegetable shortening
2 medium-size chicken breasts, skinned and washed
3 chicken thighs, skinned and washed
3 chicken legs, skinned and washed
salt and pepper to taste

1. In a large mixing bowl, beat eggs with a fork and add milk. Fill a separate mixing bowl with flour.
2. Heat shortening, preferably in an electric skillet, until it reaches 400 degrees F, then reduce heat to 350 degrees F. You should have 2 to 3 inches of hot oil in the skillet when it reaches the desired temperature.
3. Immerse each piece of chicken individually into the egg and milk mixture and then the flour, coating heavily with flour. Then put the chicken into the hot oil. Once the skillet is full, season with salt and pepper and cover with a lid.
4. Monitor the chicken constantly, turning two or three times to prevent burning on both sides. After a few minutes at the higher temperature, reduce to about 350 degrees F and allow

the chicken to cook thoroughly until dark golden brown. Total cooking time for each piece needs to be 30 to 40 minutes.

5. As each piece turns crispy and golden brown, remove it onto a paper towel to drain excess oil.

Gail's Chicken Parmesan

This is a new recipe in our family but an immediate favorite.
Serves 6
1 1/2 cups Italian Progresso bread crumbs
1/2 cup freshly grated Parmesan cheese
1/2 to 1 teaspoon kosher salt
1 teaspoon pepper
3 large chicken breasts, skinned, deboned, and split into two pieces each
1 1/2 to 2 sticks butter, melted

1. Preheat oven to 350 degrees F.
2. In a large bowl, combine bread crumbs, Parmesan, salt, and pepper.
3. Dip chicken breasts into melted butter and then into bread crumbs, covering heavily.
4. Place chicken in a baking dish and bake uncovered for 30 to 40 minutes.

Tip: The chicken can be prepared the day before and refrigerated before baking. It freezes well before or after baking. To reheat after thawing, bake in a 325 degree oven until hot.

Turkey and Cornbread Dressing

I do not have a recipe for turkey and dressing. The first year David and I were married, we were not able to be at home with family, so to follow the traditions of our families, I wanted to make a turkey.

When I called Mother to ask her how to do it, she said she would put the directions in the mail to me. The following is her essay, "On Baking the Turkey." I have pulled her handwritten copy (in her signature green ink) from my recipe files every year since 1965, when I baked my first Thanksgiving turkey.

On Baking the Turkey

If the fowl is frozen, put it out to thaw twenty-four hours ahead of when you plan to bake it. Wash it off in cold water and clean it well. Rub it with a small amount of salt. Place in roaster with about a quart of cold water. (Watch for time on the wrappings.) I usually turn oven on about midnight and let it cook at 300 degrees until about 6 a.m. (that is for an 18 to 20 pound turkey). Put a lid on the roaster and it will steam. Take it out of the oven and put it on a meat board.

Make the dressing from toasted whole wheat bread. Crumble into a bowl and add one batch of corn bread. Add five or six eggs, 1 cup of diced celery, and 1 cup of diced onions that have been sautéed in butter over medium heat. Season with pepper, rubbed sage, and salt to taste. Pour broth from the turkey pan over your dressing. You may have to add boiling water to make it soupy, and let it set 2 hours before baking. Bake an hour or longer at 400 degrees.

To make gravy, pour part of broth in a medium-sized pan; add water, butter, and a little yellow food coloring. Cut up giblets and add them. Broth can be taken from the separate cooking of the giblets. Thicken with flour or cornstarch, and add water as needed to get it to the right consistency. Bring to a boil at medium high temperature and remove from the heat. Salt and pepper to taste.

Slice turkey and put on a platter to serve, dark meat on one side, white meat on the other, with parsley around the edges.

Note: Mother's instructions were for an 18 to 20 pound turkey. Our first Thanksgiving after getting married, we had no need for such a large turkey. She must have had an afterthought, because the last paragraph of her essay read, "Look up dressing recipes for amount to make for number you are serving. The equivalent of a small loaf of bread and a batch of corn bread would make enough for you."

Summer Hot Dogs with Kraut

Serves 4 to 6
1 package hot dogs
1 (15-ounce) can sauerkraut
1/2 pound bacon
1 to 2 cups barbecue sauce

1. Split hot dogs open vertically 3/4 of the way and stuff with sauerkraut.
2. Wrap one piece of bacon around each hot dog and secure with toothpicks. Cover with barbecue sauce.
3. Grill until the hot dog and sauerkraut are brown and crispy.

Easy, Easy Salmon Cakes

Makes 4 cakes
1 (15-ounce) can processed salmon
1 egg
15 saltine crackers (more if needed)
1 teaspoon lemon juice
1/4 teaspoon Mrs. Dash
salt and pepper
1 teaspoon olive oil

1. In a large bowl, combine salmon and egg.
2. Crumble saltine crackers into bowl and mix together. Mixture should be firm enough to form patties.

3. Add lemon juice, Mrs. Dash, and salt and pepper. Form into individual cakes.
4. In a skillet greased with olive oil, fry salmon cakes over medium heat until firm and crispy.

Pot Roast

Many a Sunday when we came home from church "starving," we were greeted at the door with the wonderful aroma of pot roast. With the salad and dessert she had prepared on Saturday, Mother had Sunday dinner on the table by the time we had changed from our church clothes to our play clothes. As my children were growing up, I did the same, and we all still associate the smell of pot roast in the oven with Sunday dinner.

Serves 6 to 8
2- to 4-pound beef arm roast
1 tablespoon olive oil
1 large onion, thinly sliced
6 to 8 red potatoes, cut into chunks
1 pound carrots cut into chunks (baby peeled are a wonderful convenience)
salt and pepper

1. Preheat oven to 325 degrees F.
2. Place roast in a Dutch oven or heavy roasting pan lined with olive oil. Place onion, potatoes, and carrots on top. Add 2 to 3 cups water, then salt and pepper to taste.
3. Cover and roast for about 4 hours.

Tips:

• The water makes a good natural gravy when the roast is done. Make sure you have enough water so that it remains throughout the cooking process; this makes the roast moist. You can check it about halfway through the cooking cycle. If the water has evaporated, add more.

• This is so easy to put together, and it requires no monitoring for the four hours it is cooking. It can be prepared ahead of time and put in the refrigerator for a few hours or overnight until ready to cook.

Aunt Jewell's Chicken and Noodles

This is a century-old recipe. Aunt Jewell was taught to make this recipe by her mother-in-law, my grandmother, Ethel Rebecca (Pickett) Michel, who made it for her large family. As with most of these old recipes, it is labor-intensive, but all-natural, with none of the hidden ingredients that are found in processed foods today. The recipe can easily be doubled for a large crowd.

Makes 8 (8-ounce) servings
1 baking hen or whole frying chicken
2 cups chicken broth
1 bay leaf
dash of garlic powder
1/4 teaspoon salt, plus more to taste
pepper to taste
3 eggs, beaten until light and lemon-colored
3 tablespoons cream
3 cups flour
1 stick butter

1. In a large pan, cover chicken with approximately 6 quarts water. Add chicken broth and cook over medium to high heat about 40 minutes.
2. Add bay leaf, a few sprinkles of garlic powder, and salt and pepper to taste when the water is boiling.

3. Chicken is done when it is tender and falls off a meat fork easily. Let cool and remove chicken from the bone. Keep the chicken broth. This will be used for cooking the noodles.

4. In a large bowl, beat eggs with 1/4 teaspoon salt. Add cream. Add flour 1 cup at a time and beat. Dough will be very stiff.

5. Roll out noodle dough, using additional flour sparingly if needed to make it easier to roll out. The dough needs to be dry. As you roll the dough flat, it will keep trying to shrink; keep rolling until it is very thin. Cut into circles.

6. Place dough circles on a pastry cloth or kitchen towel and allow to dry for several hours. They can be turned over periodically to dry better. After they are dry to the touch but not crisp, stack the circles of dough, roll them up, and cut to the size desired.

7. Place chicken broth over medium to high heat. Add butter. Bring broth to a boil and add noodles a few at a time. Cook at least 15 to 30 minutes, or until soft.

8. When noodles are just about done, add chicken. You can add more chicken broth as the noodles are cooking to make sure the liquid in the pan is adequate. Add salt and pepper to taste.

Oven-Baked Brisket

Makes 6 to 8 (8-ounce) servings
3- to 4-pound brisket, fat trimmed
2 tablespoons liquid smoke
2 tablespoons soy sauce
2 teaspoons celery seed
2 teaspoons ground pepper
1 1/2 teaspoons Worcestershire sauce
1 teaspoon onion salt
1 teaspoon garlic salt
1 cup (or more to taste) bottled barbeque sauce of your choice

1. Preheat oven to 300 degrees F.
2. Remove fat from brisket.
3. Place brisket in a roasting pan, bowl, or other container. Combine all remaining ingredients except barbeque sauce and pour over brisket. Marinate in refrigerator three to four hours.
4. In roasting pan or baking dish, cover brisket with foil lightly and bake for 4 to 5 hours. Cover with barbecue sauce and bake for an additional hour.

Chicken Pot Pie

Makes 8 to 10 (8-ounce) servings

Sauce:

5 tablespoons butter
1/2 cup chopped onion
4 tablespoons flour
2 cups chicken broth
salt and pepper
1/8 teaspoon celery salt
1/8 teaspoon onion salt

Topping:

2 cups flour
1/2 cup butter
1/4 cup milk
1 egg, slightly beaten
2 tablespoons baking powder
1 teaspoon salt

Assembly:

3 cups cooked chicken, cut up
1 cup cooked frozen peas
1 cup cooked diced carrots

1. Preheat oven to 400 degrees F. Lightly grease a 9-by-13 inch casserole dish.
2. *Make sauce:* In a large pot, melt butter. Add onion and cook over low heat about 10 minutes, or until soft and light brown. Add flour and stir until blended. Slowly add chicken broth and stir over low heat until thick and smooth. Season to taste with salt and pepper. Add celery salt and onion salt.
3. *Make topping:* In a saucepan, blend all ingredients. Cook over medium heat until smooth and creamy.
4. *Assemble pot pie:* In prepared casserole dish, arrange chicken meat and vegetables in layers. Cover with sauce. Pour topping over. Bake for 25 to 30 minutes.

Tip: Cream may be substituted for part of the broth in step 1.

Ozark Mountain Chili

Makes about 12 (8-ounce) servings
4 pounds ground beef
1 1/2 cups chopped onions
3 (10.5-ounce) cans tomato soup
1/2 cup flour
3 (15.5-ounce) cans chili beans in chili sauce
1/2 cup sugar
2 1/2 to 3 tablespoons chili powder
1 tablespoon salt (or to taste)
1 tablespoon pepper
few drops Worcestershire sauce

1. In a large skillet, brown ground beef and onion over medium heat until onions are soft and ground beef is no longer pink. Cook an additional 2 to 3 minutes.
2. Add soup and stir well. Reduce heat so that nothing sticks.
3. In a plastic container, combine flour and 1/2 cup water. Mix or shake until mixture is smooth, with no lumps. Add to ground beef mixture, stir well, and continue cooking.
4. Add chili beans and continue stirring. Increase heat to medium to medium high. Add sugar, chilli powder, salt, pepper, and Worcestershire sauce. Stir well and cook over medium high heat until ingredients are well blended.
5. Reduce heat to low and continue cooking an additional 1 to 1 1/2 hours over low heat. Stir occasionally to prevent sticking.

Tip: Amounts of seasoning may vary according to taste.

Meatloaf

If you use a cast iron skillet to cook the meatloaf, you may think it will be difficult to clean. Tip for cleaning it easily: fill the pan about 1/2 to 3/4 full of water and add a small amount of dish detergent. Place on the burner and heat until it boils. Use a cooking spatula to scrape the bottom and sides of your pan. Dump this mixture, wash your pan, and you no longer have a problem pan!

Makes 4 (5- to 6-ounce) servings
1 pound hamburger
3 tablespoons chopped onion
2 to 3 slices of bread, crumbled (I prefer loaf bread crumbled rather than processed bread crumbs)
1 egg
2 tablespoons milk
1/2 teaspoon salt
1/2 teaspoon ground black pepper

1/8 teaspoon garlic salt
dash of garlic powder
olive oil, for skillet
1 cup ketchup

1. In a mixing bowl, combine all ingredients except for olive oil and ketchup in order given. Mix well by hand and form into a loaf.
2. Place loaf in a cast iron skillet or heavy baking pan coated slightly with olive oil. Cover generously with ketchup. Bake for 1 hour or until a meat thermometer, when inserted, reads 160 degrees F. Let set for a few minutes and slice.

Tip: The recipe can easily be doubled for more servings.

Mima's Spaghetti

Makes 10 (8-ounce) servings
1 pound ground beef
1 small onion chopped
1 garlic clove, chopped
salt and pepper
1 to 2 teaspoons chili powder
1 (14.5-ounce) can petite diced tomatoes
1 (14.5-ounce) can tomato sauce
dash of garlic powder
dash of garlic salt
1/2 pound spaghetti

1. In an electric skillet, brown ground beef with onion and garlic. Add salt and pepper to taste.
2. Add chili powder. Cook until meat is completely browned and onions are soft.
3. Add diced tomatoes and then about 1/3 of the can of tomato sauce. Add water to the tomato sauce left in the can, filling it to

the top. Pour the diluted tomato sauce into the pan. Add another can of water until the sauce reaches your desired consistency. Season with garlic powder, garlic salt, salt, and pepper to taste.

4. Your sauce should be about 1/3 to 1/2 way up to the top of the pan. Cover and cook on medium high heat so that it comes to a boil. Reduce heat and let simmer for 20 to 30 minutes.

5. Cook spaghetti according to directions on package. Drain and add to sauce.

Tip: Depending on the number of people you want to serve, you may need to add more tomato sauce, water, and seasonings.

Chicken Casserole

Makes 8 (8-ounce) servings
2 cups cooked chicken
1 can cream of chicken soup
1 cup chopped celery
1 can cream of mushroom soup
2 to 3 cups cooked white rice
3/4 teaspoon salt
1 cup mayonnaise
3/4 teaspoon pepper
2 tablespoons chopped onions
2 tablespoons lemon juice
1 cup chicken broth
potato chips, for topping

1. Preheat oven to 400 degrees F.

2. Combine all ingredients except for potato chips in order given, mixing thoroughly. Place in a 9-by-13 inch casserole.

3. Cover with crushed potato chips. Bake for 45 minutes or until heated through and bubbling.

Cakes

The Family Top Ten, and Then Some

Waldorf Astoria Cake (Red Velvet)

If the last four generations of our family members were polled, I'm sure this would be the number-one favorite. It is the cake most frequently requested for birthdays. Don't be discouraged if the icing is not exactly what you want the first time. This recipe takes practice, but it is worth the effort.

Makes 12 servings

Cake:

3 tablespoons cocoa
2 ounces red food coloring
1 1/2 cups sugar
1/2 cup shortening
2 eggs
1 teaspoon vanilla
2 cups sifted cake flour
1 cup buttermilk
1 teaspoon baking soda
1 tablespoon distilled white vinegar

Icing:

10 tablespoons cake flour
1 cup cold milk
2 cups sugar

1 pound butter
4 teaspoons vanilla
4-5 drops red food coloring

1. Preheat oven to 350 degrees F. Flour and grease three 8-inch pans.

Make cake:

2. In a small bowl, make a paste of the cocoa and red food coloring by mixing together well. Set aside.
3. In a large mixing bowl, cream sugar and shortening. Add eggs one at a time, followed by vanilla and food-coloring paste; mix well.
4. Add cake flour alternately with buttermilk; mix well.
5. In a separate container, combine baking soda with vinegar. Pour into cake batter while mixture is still foaming.
6. Blend cake batter thoroughly in mixer and pour into prepared pans. Bake for 17 to 20 minutes or until an inserted toothpick comes out clean. Be careful not to overcook to prevent dryness. Cool completely before icing.

While cake is baking and cooling, make icing:

7. In a small saucepan, combine cake flour and milk. Cook over medium to low heat, stirring constantly, until a smooth paste forms. (To prevent scorching, I raise the pan a few inches above the burner while it is cooking so that it heats but doesn't burn from direct heat.) Stir well to get all the lumps out.
8. Cool mixture in refrigerator for 20 to 30 minutes.
9. In a large bowl, cream sugar with butter until mixture is very fine; add vanilla. Beat until smooth and fluffy. Add cooled flour paste and continue beating until smooth, up to 10 minutes to

prevent lumps in the icing. Add 4 to 5 drops of red food coloring and continue beating.

10. *Assemble cake:* Stack layers on a cake plate and add icing between each and over top and sides.

Tip: When preparing pans to make a layered cake, grease the pan with solid shortening, flour lightly, and line with waxed paper for best removal from the pan.

Hazel P.'s Chocolate Cake

This is the chocolate cake Hazel made for our Bull Creek outings and picnics.

Makes 12 servings.

Cake:

1 1/2 cups sugar
1/4 pound butter
1/2 cup cocoa
2 cups cake flour
1 teaspoon baking powder
1/2 teaspoon salt
1 teaspoon vanilla
red food coloring
1 teaspoon soda dissolved in 1 tablespoon boiling water
3 eggs whites, beaten stiff

Chocolate icing:

4 tablespoons butter
3 cups powdered sugar
1/2 cup cocoa

2 tablespoons cream

2 teaspoons vanilla

2 egg whites, beaten stiff

1. Preheat oven to 350 degrees F. Grease and flour two 8-inch cake pans.

Make cake:

2. In a large bowl, cream sugar, butter, and cocoa. Sift together flour, baking powder, and salt and add to sugar mixture.
3. Pour 1 cup water into a measuring cup and add vanilla and a few drops of red food coloring. Add to batter. Next, add soda dissolved in water. Mix well. Fold in beaten egg whites.
4. Pour batter into prepared cake pans. Bake 20 to 30 minutes, until inserted toothpick comes out clean. Cool before icing.
5. *Make icing:* Cream butter, sugar, and cocoa together. Add cream and vanilla. Fold in beaten egg whites.
6. *Assemble cake:* Place first layer on a cake plate. Top with icing and then second layer. Spread icing over top and sides.

Tip: Icing can be doubled for more generous amount.

Mom DeLair's Chocolate Cake

Good with white or chocolate frosting.

Makes 12 (6-ounce) servings

1 1/2 sticks butter (or margarine)

2 cups sugar

2 eggs

2 1/2 cups flour

1/2 cup cocoa

1/2 teaspoon salt

1 cup buttermilk

red food coloring

2 teaspoons baking soda dissolved in 1 cup boiling water

1. Preheat oven to 350 degrees F. Grease and flour three 8-inch pans.
2. In a large bowl, cream butter and sugar. Add eggs.
3. Sift together flour, cocoa, and salt. Add to sugar mixture alternately with buttermilk, then add a few drops of red food coloring. Stir in baking soda dissolved in water.
4. Pour batter into prepared pans. Bake for 20 to 25 minutes or until inserted toothpick comes out clean.

Nell's Sour Cream Cake

Makes 8-10 servings

Cake:

2 sticks butter
3 cups sugar
6 eggs
1 (8-ounce) carton sour cream
3 cups sifted cake flour
1/4 teaspoon soda

Orange glaze:

1 cup granulated sugar
1/4 cup cornstarch
1/2 teaspoon salt
1 cup fresh orange juice
1 teaspoon fresh lemon juice
2 tablespoons grated orange rind
2 tablespoons butter

1. Preheat oven to 350 degrees F. Grease and flour a 10-inch tube pan.
2. *Make cake:* In a large bowl, cream butter and sugar. Add eggs one at a time, mixing well after each egg. Cream again for a long time. Add sour cream, sifted cake flour, and soda. Mix well. Pour batter into prepared pans. Bake for 1 hour 45 minutes, or until golden brown.
3. *Make glaze:* In a saucepan, combine sugar, cornstarch, and salt. Add juices slowly and stir until smooth. Add orange rind and butter. Cook over low heat until thick and glossy.
4. Cool glaze and spread on cooled cake.

Strawberry Shortcake

This is an old-fashioned recipe and yummy!
Makes 9 (4-ounce) servings

Strawberries:

fresh strawberries, at least 1 to 2 pounds for a crowd
1 1/2 to 1 3/4 cups sugar

Shortcake:

1 1/2 cups flour
3/4 cup sugar
2 teaspoons baking powder
1/4 teaspoon salt
1 egg
1/4 cup melted butter
3/4 cup milk
1 teaspoon vanilla

For serving:

Reddi-wip or 1/2 pint fresh whipping cream

1. *Prepare strawberries:* Stem strawberries. Place in a large bowl and cover with sugar. Cover tightly and refrigerate at least 2 hours. Overnight is best.
2. Preheat oven to 350 degrees F. Grease and flour a 7- to 8-inch square baking pan.
3. *Make shortcake:* Sift dry ingredients into a large bowl. In a medium bowl, drop egg into melted butter, then add milk and vanilla. Combine the two mixtures and beat well. Pour into prepared pan and bake for about 20 minutes. Cool and cut into 9 pieces.
4. *For serving:* With an old fashioned potato masher, mash strawberries thoroughly until very juicy. Slice a piece of cake horizontally into two pieces. Put first piece in a bowl and cover with strawberries. Put second piece on top and cover with another spoonful of strawberries. Then cover with Reddi-wip or freshly whipped cream. Repeat with remaining ingredients.

Note: A variation for this one-egg cake recipe is to make an icing using a mixture of brown sugar, butter, and coconut. Mix 1 cup brown sugar, 1/2 stick butter, and 1/2 cup coconut over medium to high heat until it reaches a boiling point. Remove from heat, cool slightly, and spread over cake.

Auntie's Italian Coconut Cake

Makes 12 (5-ounce) servings

Cake:

2 sticks butter
2 cups sugar

5 eggs, separated
2 cups sifted flour
1 teaspoon soda
1 cup buttermilk
1 teaspoon vanilla
2 cups shredded coconut
1/2 to 1 cup nuts (pecans or walnuts)

Icing:

1 stick butter
1 (8-ounce) package cream cheese
1 teaspoon vanilla
1 box powdered sugar

1. Preheat oven to 350 degrees F. Grease and flour three 8-inch layer pans.

Make cake:

2. Cream together butter, sugar, and egg yolks (whites will be used later). Stir in sifted flour and soda alternately with buttermilk. Add vanilla, coconut, and nuts.
3. In a separate bowl, beat egg whites until they form stiff peaks. Fold into batter.
4. Pour into prepared pans and bake for 25 to 35 minutes, until an inserted tooth pick comes out clean.
5. *Make icing:* In a medium bowl, combine all ingredients. Mix well and spread over cooled cake.

Tip: For a more generous amount of icing, the recipe can be doubled.

Sherry's Italian Cream Cake

Makes 12 (4-ounce) servings

Cake:

1 cup buttermilk
1 teaspoon soda
2 cups sugar
1 stick butter
1/2 cup shortening
5 eggs, separated
2 cups flour
1 teaspoon vanilla
1 small can flaked coconut
1 cup chopped pecans or walnuts

Icing:

8 ounces cream cheese
1 stick butter, softened
1 pound box sifted powdered sugar
1 teaspoon vanilla
chopped pecans or walnuts (optional)

1. Preheat oven to 325 degrees F. Grease and flour two 8-inch layer pans.

Make cake:

2. In a small bowl, combine buttermilk and soda.
3. In a large bowl, cream sugar, butter, and shortening, Add egg yolks one at a time and beat well.

4. Add buttermilk mixture and flour alternately to sugar mixture. Add vanilla.
5. In a separate bowl, beat egg whites until they form stiff peaks. Fold into batter. Add coconut and nuts.
6. Pour batter into prepared pans and bake for 20 to 25 minutes.
7. *Make icing*: Mix cream cheese, softened butter, powdered sugar, vanilla, and nuts, if desired. Spread over cooled cake.

Apricot Cake

Nice for a festive breakfast or brunch.
Makes 12 (4- to 5-ounce) servings
3/4 cup Wesson oil
2 cups sugar, plus 1 teaspoon
3 eggs
2 jars apricot baby food
2 cups flour
1 teaspoon baking powder
1/2 teaspoon salt
2 teaspoons cinnamon, divided
1 cup chopped nuts

1. Lightly grease a Bundt pan.
2. In a large bowl, mix together oil, 2 cups of the sugar, and eggs. Then add baby food, flour, baking powder, and salt. Mix well and add 1 teaspoon cinnamon and chopped nuts.
3. Make a mixture of 1 teaspoon sugar and 1 teaspoon cinnamon and sprinkle in bottom of prepared pan. Pour batter into pan. Put in a cold oven and set oven temperature to 300 degrees F. Bake for 1 hour 15 minutes.

Hummingbird Cake

This recipe was not original with Mother. She took it from *Southern Living* magazine in the 1970s, and it has been passed down.

Makes 12 (5-ounce) servings

Cake:

3 cups all-purpose flour
2 cups sugar
1 teaspoon baking soda
1 teaspoon ground cinnamon
1/2 teaspoon salt
3 eggs, beaten
3/4 cup vegetable oil
1 1/2 teaspoons vanilla extract
1 (8-ounce) can crushed pineapple, undrained
1 cup chopped pecans
1 3/4 cups mashed bananas
1/2 cup chopped pecans

Cream cheese frosting:

1/2 cup butter or margarine, softened
1 (8-ounce) package cream cheese, softened
1 (16-ounce) package powdered sugar, sifted
1 teaspoon vanilla extract

1. Preheat oven to 350 degrees F. Grease and flour three 9-inch round pans.

Make cake:

2. In a large bowl, combine and sift first 5 ingredients. Add eggs and oil, stirring until dry ingredients are moistened. Do not beat.
3. Stir in vanilla, pineapple, pecans, and bananas.
4. Pour batter into prepared pans. Bake until a wooden pick inserted in center comes out clean. Cool in pans.
5. *Make icing:* Cream butter and softened cream cheese. Gradually add powdered sugar; beat until light and fluffy. Stir in vanilla.
6. Remove cake from pans and apply icing.

Willie Cake

This cake is good as dessert or a coffee cake for special-occasion breakfasts.
Makes 12 (5- to 6-ounce) servings
1 box Golden Butter Cake Mix
1 (8-ounce) carton sour cream
3/4 cup Wesson oil
1/2 cup sugar
3 eggs, at room temperature
2 tablespoons brown sugar
2 teaspoons cinnamon
1/3 cup chopped pecans

1. Preheat oven to 375 degrees F. Grease and flour a Bundt pan.
2. In a large bowl, mix together first 5 ingredients until well blended (do not beat very long). Pour half of batter into prepared pan.
3. In a small bowl, mix together brown sugar, cinnamon, and chopped pecans.
4. Sprinkle pecan mixture over batter in pan. Top with remaining batter. Bake for about 45 minutes.

Carrot Cake

Makes 12 (5-ounce) servings

Cake:

1 1/2 cups Wesson oil
2 cups sugar
4 eggs
2 cups sifted cake flour
2 teaspoons baking powder
2 teaspoons soda
2 teaspoons cinnamon
1 teaspoon salt
3 cups shredded carrots
1 cup chopped walnuts

Icing:

1 (8-ounce) package Philadelphia Cream Cheese
1/2 stick butter
2 teaspoons vanilla
1 box powdered sugar

1. Preheat oven to 350 degrees F. Grease and flour three 8-inch pans, and line with waxed paper.

Make cake:

2. In a large bowl, combine oil and sugar and cream well. Add eggs, one at a time.
3. In a medium bowl, sift together flour, baking powder, soda, cinnamon, and salt. Add to creamed mixture and beat well.

4. Add shredded carrots and walnuts. Beat until all ingredients are blended thoroughly.
5. Pour batter into prepared pans. Bake for 25 minutes or until inserted toothpick comes out clean.
6. *Make icing:* In a medium bowl, combine all ingredients and beat until smooth and creamy.
7. *Assemble cake:* Place one layer of cooled cake on a cake plate. Spread top with icing. Add second layer and ice. Finally, add the third layer, ice it and the sides.

Note: Our family desires more icing than this provides, so an alternative recipe provides ample icing for in-between layers: Beat together 2 large packages cream cheese, 2 sticks butter, 3 teaspoons vanilla, and 3 boxes powdered sugar. Beat until smooth and creamy. Decadent, but delicious.

Chocolate Buttermilk Cake

This has been a family favorite for decades and is great for serving large crowds. The size of the cookie sheet can vary.

Makes approximately 20 (2 1/2-inch) squares

Cake:

2 cups flour
2 cups sugar
2 sticks margarine or butter
4 tablespoons cocoa
1 teaspoon soda
1/2 cup buttermilk
1 teaspoon vanilla
2 eggs

Frosting:

1 stick margarine or butter
3 tablespoons cocoa
3 tablespoons milk
1/2 package powdered sugar
dash vanilla

1. Preheat oven to 350 degrees F. Grease and flour a 10-by-15-inch cookie sheet.

Make cake:

2. In a large bowl, sift together flour and sugar.
3. In a saucepan, combine 1 cup water, margarine or butter, and cocoa. Bring to a boil over medium to high heat and add to flour and sugar mixture. Beat well.
4. Dissolve soda in buttermilk and pour into mixture. Add vanilla and eggs and continue beating a few more minutes until smooth.
5. Pour onto prepared cookie sheet and bake for 25 to 30 minutes or until inserted toothpick comes out clean.

Make frosting:

6. In a saucepan, combine margarine or butter, cocoa, and milk. Bring to boil over high heat. Remove from heat.
7. In a mixing bowl, combined powdered sugar and a dash of vanilla. Blend in heated ingredients. Beat until smooth and creamy. Ice cake while it is still warm.

Banana Split Cake

This recipe, too, is an all-time family favorite and has been handed down to the third generation of family members. It is great for showers, luncheons, and gatherings of any kind. When I have served it at ladies' luncheons, I have actually had guests ask for a second piece. What a compliment to the hostess!

Makes 16 (3- to 4-ounce) squares
2 to 3 cups graham cracker crumbs
2 eggs
2 sticks butter, softened
1 pound box powdered sugar
6 bananas, thinly sliced
1 (15-ounce) can crushed pineapple, well drained
1 pound fresh strawberries, thinly sliced
2 packages Dream Whip, prepared according to package directions
1 cup milk
1/4 cup chopped pecans

1. Prepare a graham cracker crust according to directions on box and pat into a 9-by-13-inch dish. Refrigerate for at least 1 hour.
2. In a mixer, combine eggs, softened butter, and powdered sugar. Beat well until mixture is smooth and creamy.
3. Cover base layer of graham cracker crust with thin slices of banana. Top with pineapple. Cover pineapple with sliced strawberries.
4. Spread prepared Dream Whip on top. Sprinkle chopped pecans over. Refrigerate until served.
5. Cut into squares for serving.

Grandma Louise's Strawberry Angel Food Cake Supreme

Great for spring meals, Easter dinner, or any special occasion.

Makes 12 (5- to 6-ounce) servings.

For cake:

2 cups sugar
1 2/3 cups cake flour
15 egg whites brought to room temperature (brown eggs preferred)
1/4 cup cold water
2 1/2 teaspoons cream of tartar
1 teaspoon vanilla

For filling and icing:

2 (6-ounce) packages strawberry Jell-O
2 cups boiling water
1 (16-ounce) package sliced frozen strawberries with natural juice
1 quart whipping cream

Make cake:

1. Preheat oven to 375 degrees F. Grease and flour a 10-inch angel food cake pan.
2. Sift sugar and cake flour together ten times. Set aside.
3. In a large mixing bowl, combine egg whites with cold water and beat until fluffy. Add cream of tartar and continue beating. Add vanilla and beat until very stiff *but not dry.*
4. With an old-fashioned flat wire whip, fold flour mixture into egg mixture, a little at a time.
5. Pour into prepared pan. Run a rubber spatula through the mixture two or three times very easily. Bake for 45 minutes. Cake will be tall.
6. Turn upside down and let set several hours. Peel brown off top, then take out of pan by running a rubber spatula around sides of cake carefully. Let set overnight before slicing.

Fill and ice:

7. Dissolve Jell-O in boiling water. Cool. Add frozen strawberries with natural juice. Let mixture thicken and become ropey.
8. In a large bowl, beat whipping cream until stiff. Then add strawberry and Jell-O mixture. Blend well.
9. Slice angel food cake horizontally into three layers. Put bottom layer on a cake plate and spread with filling. Add next two layers likewise. Then spread remaining filling all over sides and top and inside center.
10. Keep covered in the refrigerator. Will be good for a week or more, if it lasts that long!

Tip: Special note from Grandma Louise: "Once you start beating egg whites, don't stop for anything until cake is in oven."

Applesauce Cake

This recipe is one of the really old ones, and Mother served it on Thanksgiving when we had huge crowds of people.

Makes 15 to 20 squares, depending on size cut

Cake:

3/4 cup white sugar
3/4 cup brown sugar
3/4 cup solid vegetable shortening
2 cups applesauce
2 eggs
2 1/2 cups flour
1/2 teaspoon cinnamon
1/2 teaspoon cloves
1/2 teaspoon allspice

1/2 teaspoon salt

2 teaspoons soda dissolved in 1/4 cup warm water

1 teaspoon vanilla

1 cup raisins, fluffed in a small amount of butter and water until slightly warmed, then drained

Icing:

1 cup brown sugar

1/2 cup half and half

pinch of soda

1 cup raisins

1 cup black walnuts

1. Preheat oven to 350 degrees F. Flour and grease a cookie sheet.

Make cake:

2. In a large bowl, cream sugars and shortening. Add vanilla, applesauce and eggs.
3. Sift together and add dry ingredients to sugar mixture in order given. Fold raisins into batter, and soda dissolved in warm water. Beat well.
4. Pour onto prepared cookie sheet and bake for 25 to 30 minutes or until pick inserted in the center comes out clean.
5. *Make icing:* In a saucepan over medium to high heat, combine brown sugar and half and half. Stir until smooth and discontinue stirring when mixture boils. Add a pinch of soda and 1 cup raisins. Cook until soft ball stage. Beat after taking off stove and add 1 cup nuts.
6. Spread icing on cooled cake.

Note: Recipe can be halved and baked in a 9-by-13-inch pan for a more traditional-size cake.

Ambrosia Cake

In addition to the Red Velvet Cake, this was a favorite for birthdays in our family.

Makes 12 (5-ounce) servings

Cake:

1 deluxe Duncan Heinz yellow cake mix (or make your own from scratch)
1 egg

Clear orange filling:

1 cup sugar
4 tablespoons cornstarch
1/4 teaspoon salt
1 cup fresh orange juice
2 tablespoons lemon juice
2 tablespoons butter
2 tablespoons grated orange rind

Fluffy white icing:

1 cup sugar
1/3 cup cold water
1/3 teaspoon cream of tartar
3 egg whites
1 teaspoon vanilla

For assembly:

fresh coconut

1. *Make cake:* Prepare cake mix as directed on box, adding 1 extra egg to mix. Bake in three 8-inch layer pans; cool.
2. *Make clear orange filling:* Meanwhile, in a heavy saucepan, combine sugar, cornstarch, and salt. Mix well. Add 1 cup orange juice a little at a time; mix until smooth. Add lemon juice, butter, and grated orange rind. Bring to a boil over medium heat; boil 1 minute or until clear. Set aside to cool.

Make icing:

3. In a heavy saucepan, combine sugar, cold water, and cream of tartar. Put lid on saucepan and cook for 3 minutes. While syrup cooks, beat 3 egg whites until stiff peaks form.
4. After syrup has cooked 3 minutes, take lid off. Cook, without stirring, until a 6- to 8-inch thread can be formed using a wooden spoon.
5. Pour syrup over egg whites in a thin stream, beating constantly. Add vanilla.

Assemble cake:

6. When cake layers and orange filling are cool, stack 1 layer on top of the other with filling between, saving enough to put over top layer.
7. When frosting holds its shape, spread over cake. Immediately cover sides and top with fresh coconut.

Aunt Virginia's German Chocolate Cake

Most of these cakes require considerable time in the kitchen, but when prepared for your favorite people, they are an expression of love. Note that some people say *icing* and some say *frosting.* I've never known the difference. In the Ozarks, we mostly say *icing.*

Makes 12 (5- to 6-ounce) servings

Cake:

2 cups sugar
1 cup shortening
4 egg yolks, beaten
1 cup buttermilk with 1 teaspoon soda dissolved in it
1 package German chocolate (Baker's), melted in 1 cup boiling water
1 teaspoon vanilla
dash salt
2 1/2 cups sifted cake flour
4 egg whites, beaten

Frosting:

3/4 stick butter or margarine
1 1/2 cups sugar
3/4 pint whipping cream
4 egg yolks
1 1/2 cups coconut
1 1/2 cups pecans
1 teaspoon vanilla

1. Preheat oven to 350 degrees F. Grease and flour three 8-inch cake pans.
2. *Make cake:* In a large bowl, cream sugar and shortening. Add beaten egg yolks. Add buttermilk with soda dissolved in it. Add chocolate squares melted in boiling water. Add vanilla, salt, and flour. Mix well. Fold in egg whites. Bake in prepared pans until inserted toothpick comes out clean.
3. *Make frosting:* In a large saucepan over medium to high heat, cook butter, sugar, vanilla, and whipping cream and bring to a boil. Add small amount of hot mixture to beaten yolks. Then

combine remaining hot mixture with egg yolks and cook slowly until glossy and clear. Add coconut and pecans.

4. Allow cake and frosting to cool completely before putting frosting on cake.

Pies and Cobblers

Mother's As-Usual Pie Crust

Makes enough for a 1-crust pie or cobbler.
1 1/2 cups flour
1 teaspoon salt
1 teaspoon sugar
smidgen baking powder (less than 1/8 teaspoon)
3/4 cup vegetable shortening
1/3 to 1/2 cup ice water

1. Place flour in a large bowl. Add salt, sugar, and baking powder and mix together.
2. Add shortening to flour mixture and cut with a fork until crumbly. Add ice water and form into a ball. Add water until the dough is sticky.
3. Spread waxed paper on countertop and sprinkle thoroughly with flour. Cover rolling pin with flour as well. Place ball of dough on waxed paper and roll to thickness desired for pie or cobbler. It may be necessary to add flour to the dough so that it is of rolling consistency.

Never-Fail Pie Crust

Makes enough for 2 pies
3 cups flour
1 teaspoon salt
1 1/4 cups shortening
1 egg, slightly beaten
5 tablespoons ice water
1 teaspoon vinegar

1. Sift flour and salt into a large bowl. Add shortening and mix well with a pastry mixer or fork.
2. Add beaten egg, ice water, and vinegar. Mix thoroughly with fork or pastry mixer and roll out.
3. Make four crusts. Do not use hands any more than necessary.

Granny Lillian's Paper-Sack Apple Pie

Makes 8 (5-ounce) slices
1 unbaked pie crust
6 to 8 Granny Smith apples, sliced
1/2 cup sugar
1/2 cup flour
2/3 stick butter
1 teaspoon cinnamon
1 large brown paper bag

1. Preheat oven to 400 degrees F.
2. Prepare a pie dish with a bottom unbaked pie crust. Add apples, abundantly filling the unbaked crust.
3. In a medium bowl, combine sugar and flour; spread over apples. Dot with butter. Sprinkle with cinnamon. (This is the top crust.)
4. Place pie in a large brown paper bag and bake for 10 minutes. Then turn oven down and bake very slowly for 2 hours more at 325 degrees F.

Mother's Peach Cobbler

There was never a recipe for this dessert. When I got married, Mother had to write it based on her process, so there are many variables. The amounts of sugar and butter can be adjusted to suit individual tastes. Prepare Mother's As-Usual Pie Crust, roll it out, and have it ready to place on top of the fruit as soon as it is in the baking dish.

Makes 15 (4- to 5-ounce) servings
15 to 20 average-size fresh peaches, sliced
1 1/2 to 1 3/4 cups sugar
3 heaping tablespoons flour
3/4 stick butter
Mother's As-Usual Pie Crust, prepared

1. Preheat oven to 475 degrees F.
2. Fill 9-by-13-inch baking dish abundantly with sliced peaches.
3. In a medium bowl, mix sugar and flour. When mixed well, pour over fruit. Add about 3/4 stick butter cut into squares over top of the fruit and flour mixture. Place crust on top. If it covers the fruit tightly, poke plenty of holes in the dough. It needs to breathe.
4. Bake until bubbling and browned on top, 35 to 40 minutes. Watch carefully so that it does not burn.

Note: Blackberries or apples can be used in place of peaches.

Annabelle's Pecan Pie

Makes 8 (5-ounce) slices
1 unbaked pie crust
1/4 cup butter
1 cup light brown sugar
1 cup white corn syrup
1/4 teaspoon salt
3 eggs
1 teaspoon vanilla
1 cup chopped pecans

1. Preheat oven to 350 degrees F. Line a 9-inch pan with unbaked pie crust.
2. In a medium bowl, cream butter, sugar, and syrup.

3. In a separate bowl, add salt to eggs and beat until light and fluffy. Then add to butter mixture. Stir in vanilla and nuts.
4. Pour filling into prepared pan. Bake for 50 minutes.

Mom DeLair's Pecan Pie

Makes 8 (5-ounce) slices
unbaked pastry for one 9-inch pie pan
3 eggs
2/3 cup sugar
1 1/4 cups of Mrs. Butterworth's syrup
1 cup coarsely chopped pecans

1. Preheat oven to 375 degrees F. Line 9-inch pie pan with unbaked pastry.
2. In a large bowl, combine eggs, sugar, and syrup. Beat with an electric mixer.
3. Add pecans and blend well. Pour into pastry-lined pie pan. Bake for 40 to 45 minutes.

Note: If pie browns too quickly, lay a piece of foil loosely over the pie.

Grandma Gertie's Pumpkin Pie

Makes 8 (5-ounce) slices
2/3 cup sugar
2 teaspoons pumpkin pie spice
1/2 teaspoon salt
1 cup packed brown sugar
1 tablespoon molasses
1 (16-ounce) can pumpkin
1 (12-ounce) can evaporated milk
2 eggs, slightly beaten
1 (9-inch) pie crust

whipped cream, for serving

1. Preheat oven to 425 degrees F.
2. In a large bowl, sift together sugar, spice, and salt.
3. Add brown sugar and molasses. Add pumpkin and mix well. Add milk and continue beating.
4. Add slightly beaten eggs and beat lightly.
5. Put mixture in pie shell and bake 15 minutes. Then reduce heat to 350 degrees F and continue baking for 45 minutes.
6. Serve topped with whipped cream.

Rhubarb Cobbler

Our family did not eat rhubarb, but it is a favorite of many Ozarkians. Mother had this recipe, cut from the *Springfield News Leader*, in her large recipe collection.

Makes 15 (4-ounce) serving
2 cups sugar, divided
1 cup flour
2 teaspoons baking powder
2 tablespoons shortening
3/4 cup milk
3/4 teaspoon salt
1 teaspoon vanilla
3 cups rhubarb, cut up
1 cup hot water

1. Preheat oven to 400 F degrees. Grease and flour a 9-by-13-inch baking dish.
2. In a large bowl, combine 1 cup sugar, flour, baking powder, shortening, milk, salt, and vanilla. Mix well.
3. Spread dough in bottom of prepared baking dish. Sprinkle rhubarb over. Sprinkle 1 cup sugar over rhubarb. Add hot water.

4. Bake for 15 minutes; reduce heat and bake at 350 degrees F for 35 minutes. The crust should bubble up around the rhubarb.
5. Serve with ice cream.

Strawberry Pie

Yields 16 (3- to 4-ounce) squares
1/2 cup butter
1/4 cup brown sugar
1 cup flour
1/2 cup chopped pecans
1/2 pint whipping cream
1 (16-ounce) bag frozen strawberries, partially thawed
1 cup sugar
1 tablespoon lemon juice
2 egg whites

1. Preheat oven to 400 degrees F. Grease and flour a 10-by-15-inch cookie sheet.
2. In a large bowl, mix together butter, brown sugar, flour, and pecans. Place on prepared cookie sheet. Bake until golden brown, about 15 minutes, stirring often. Outside edges will brown first.
3. When done, place half the baked crust (crumbled) on the bottom of a 9-by-13 inch baking dish. Reserve half to put on top later.
4. In a medium bowl, whip whipping cream. Set aside.
5. In a large bowl, mix together strawberries, sugar, lemon juice, and egg whites. Beat for 20 minutes until frothy and stiff. Fold in whipped cream.
6. Place mixture in baking dish on top of crust. Sprinkle remaining crust mixture (crumbled) on top and freeze for several hours.
7. Remove from freezer a few minutes before serving.

Debbie's Buttermilk Pie

Makes 8 (5-ounce) servings
3 3/4 cups sugar
1/2 cup flour
1 teaspoon salt
1 cup margarine, melted
6 eggs
1 cup buttermilk
1 teaspoon vanilla
2 unbaked pie shells

1. Preheat oven to 375 degrees F.
2. In a large bowl, combine sugar, flour, and salt. Add margarine and eggs. Beat slightly.
3. Add buttermilk. Spoon-beat until thoroughly mixed.
4. Pour filling into unbaked pie shells and bake for 40 to 45 minutes.

Note: The recipe can be halved to make just one pie.

Mother's Custard Pie

Makes 8 (5-ounce) servings
2 2/3 cups hot milk (not boiling)
1 cup sugar
1 teaspoon vanilla
3 eggs, slightly beaten
9-inch unbaked pie crust

1. Preheat oven to 450 degrees F.
2. In a large bowl, mix together milk, sugar, and vanilla.
3. Add slightly beaten eggs and combine. Pour into pie crust.

4. Bake for 10 minutes. Reduce heat to 350 degrees F and bake another 30 minutes.

Coconut Cream Pie

Makes 8 (4- to 5-ounce) servings
2/3 cup sugar
1/2 teaspoon salt
3 tablespoons cornstarch
2 tablespoons flour
3 cups milk
3 egg yolks, slightly beaten
1 tablespoon butter
1 1/2 teaspoons vanilla
1/2 pint fresh whipping cream
1/2 cup coconut
1 baked pie crust
sweetened whipped cream, for serving
toasted coconut, for serving

1. In a saucepan, combine sugar, salt, cornstarch, and flour. Gradually stir in milk and cook over moderate heat, stirring constantly, until mixture thickens and boils. Boil 1 minute. Remove from heat.
2. Stir a little of the mixture into the egg yolks. Blend into hot mixture in saucepan. Boil one minute more, stirring constantly. Remove from heat.
3. Blend in butter and vanilla. Cool, stirring occasionally.
4. Pour into cooled pie crust and chill for 2 hours.
5. Top with sweetened whipped cream, sprinkle with toasted coconut, and keep refrigerated. Remove from refrigerator 20 minutes before serving.

Ginny's Fudge Pie

Makes 8 (4- to 5-ounce) servings
1/2 cup butter
1 cup sugar
2 egg yolks
2 squares dark chocolate
1/2 cup flour
1 teaspoon vanilla
1/8 teaspoon salt
2 egg whites
1 unbaked pie crust

1. Preheat oven to 325 degrees F.
2. In a large bowl, beat butter until partially soft. Gradually beat in sugar until creamy. Beat in egg yolks.
3. Melt chocolate over hot water and cool slightly. Beat into mixture. Add flour, vanilla, and salt.
4. Beat egg whites until stiff. Fold into batter.
5. Pour filling into unbaked pie shell and bake for 30 minutes.
6. Serve with whipped cream or vanilla ice cream on top.

Ten-Cent Bar Chocolate Pie

Makes 8 (5-ounce) servings
1 baked graham cracker pie crust
1 cup miniature marshmallows
1/2 cup milk
4 (1.55-ounce) ten-cent Hershey bars (1969 price)
whipped cream, for serving

1. Follow package directions for preparing graham cracker pie crust and bake.

2. In a double boiler (or over hot water), melt marshmallows, milk and Hershey bars. Stir well, turning often with a spatula. Remove from heat and pour into crust.
3. Chill in refrigerator for several hours before serving. Top with whipped cream.

Vintage Salads, Vegetables, and Desserts

*A Few of Our Favorite Things That Still Taste
Good in the Twenty-First Century*

Salads

Mother's Easy Potato Salad

This is the recipe we *always* made when we had picnics at Bull Creek. Once the picnic was set, Mother could whip it up in less than an hour, enough to feed a dozen people or more and still have some left over.

Makes 20 5-ounce servings
5 pounds Russet potatoes with skin on, boiled and cooled
4 to 6 eggs, hard-boiled and cooled, shells removed
1 (10-ounce) jar sweet pickle relish, drained
1 cup real mayonnaise
2 tablespoons mustard
1 teaspoon sugar
1 tablespoon milk
1/2 teaspoon white vinegar
1 teaspoon salt
1 teaspoon ground white pepper
1/2 teaspoon celery salt

1 teaspoon celery seed
dash of paprika
green olives with pimento stuffing (optional)

1. In a large bowl, peel potatoes and cut into small chunks. Dice eggs and add to potatoes. Add drained relish.
2. In a medium bowl, mix mayonnaise, mustard, sugar, milk, and vinegar until smooth and creamy. Add to potato mixture along with salt, pepper, and celery salt and celery seed to taste.
3. When potato salad has been transferred to a serving dish, sprinkle with paprika. I sometimes slice olives thinly and place on top of the salad to garnish.

Note: There was never a recipe for this potato salad. Amounts of ingredients can be adjusted to suit individual tastes. That's how my sisters and I learned to cook. In a recent conversation with Sherry, I asked her how many potatoes she uses when she makes potato salad. She answered, "I fill up my pot." We learned to add a little more of whatever to get the desired amount, because amounts will vary depending on number of people you want to serve.

Aunt Rose's German Potato Salad

Aunt Rose could be counted on to bring this scrumptious dish to family gatherings. She and Uncle Exie had met in Mannheim, Germany; he'd landed on Omaha Beach on D-Day and eventually found himself in Mannheim with his army unit. He brought Aunt Rose to the homestead in 1947 as his war bride. She immediately endeared herself to the Michel family, became a proud American citizen, and was loved by her many nieces and nephews.

Makes 15 6-ounce servings
4 pounds Idaho baking potatoes, scrubbed
1 tablespoon unsalted butter

1 pound bacon, cut into ¼-inch cubes
2 medium onions, chopped
2 garlic cloves, minced
1 1/2 cups chicken broth, more if needed
1/3 cup white vinegar
1/2 cup minced fresh parsley, divided
salt and pepper, to taste

1. Put potatoes in large pot of cold salted water. Bring to a boil over moderately high heat and cook, partially covered, until tender when pierced with a fork, 30 to 40 minutes. Drain and let cool.
2. In a skillet, melt butter over moderately high heat. Add bacon and cook, stirring occasionally, until crisp, about 5 minutes.
3. Reduce heat to moderate and add onions and garlic to the bacon and fat in the skillet. Cook until onions are softened but not browned, 8 to 10 minutes.
4. Add chicken broth and vinegar. Increase heat to moderately high and bring dressing to a boil. Remove from heat.
5. Peel cooked potatoes and cut into ½-inch cubes. In a large bowl, combine potatoes and dressing and toss to mix. Season with 1/4 of the minced parsley and salt and pepper to taste.
6. Turn the potato salad into a serving bowl and garnish with remaining chopped parsley.

Five-Cup Salad

This became popular in the early fifties, and it was a standby for me as a young bride in the sixties. Easy and tasty!

Makes 4 to 6 (6-ounce) servings
1 cup pineapple chunks
1 cup mandarin oranges
1 cup sour cream
1 cup miniature marshmallows

1 cup fresh coconut

In a large serving bowl, mix together all ingredients. Refrigerate at least two hours until ready to serve.

Aunt Libby's Cole Slaw

Makes 12 (4- to 6-ounce) servings
2 medium heads cabbage, finely shredded
2 red onions, finely sliced
2 teaspoons salt
1 cup oil
1 cup white vinegar
7/8 cup sugar
1 teaspoon celery seed

1. In a large bowl, combine cabbage, onions, and salt.
2. In a saucepan, combine oil, vinegar, sugar, and celery seed. Bring to a rolling boil and pour over cabbage mixture.
3. Let stand 2 hours. Mix well and refrigerate several hours before serving.

Three-Bean Salad

Makes 8 to 10 (6-ounce) servings

Salad:

1 15-ounce can cut green beans, drained
1 15-ounce can wax beans, drained
1 15-ounce can large kidney beans, drained and washed
1 large green pepper, chopped to desired size
1 medium red or white onion, chopped to desired size
1 4-ounce jar ripe pimento, chopped to desired size

Dressing:

3/4 cup sugar
2/3 cup apple cider vinegar
1/3 cup vegetable oil
1 teaspoon salt
1/2 teaspoon pepper
dash garlic salt

1. *Make the salad:* In a large bowl, combine beans, green pepper, onion, and pimento.
2. *Make the dressing:* In a small bowl, whisk all ingredients until thoroughly blended.
3. Pour dressing over vegetables. Let stand overnight. Drain off liquid before serving.

Note: Keep the drained-off liquid in case there is salad left. It will keep in the refrigerator for quite some time if excess dressing is added back.

Fresh Broccoli Salad

Makes 8 (6-ounce) servings
2 broccoli heads, florets only
1 pound bacon, cooked, chopped, and drained
1 cup raisins
1/2 cup slivered almonds (optional)
1 small red onion, diced
1 cup mayonnaise
3/4 cup sugar
2 tablespoons vinegar

1. In a large mixing bowl, combine broccoli, bacon, raisins, almonds, and onion.

2. In a small bowl, combine mayonnaise, sugar, and vinegar. Mix well and add to broccoli mixture. Mix and refrigerate for several hours before serving.

Congealed Salads

During the fifties and sixties, congealed salads were very popular. They came in every color imaginable, depending on the flavor of Jell-O called for in the recipe. Mother had dozens of recipes for Jell-O salads. Many of them were tasty, but they lost their popularity during subsequent decades. It seems that some of those recipes might be worth resurrecting in the twenty-first century. Some that we had for holiday dinners were especially yummy!

Yum-Yum Salad

Because of its yellow color, this is a delightful recipe to serve for Easter.

Makes 8 (6-ounce) servings
1 (15-ounce) can crushed pineapple
3/4 cup sugar
1 envelope lemon Jell-O
1/2 cup cold water
1 cup heavy whipping cream
1/2 cup chopped nuts
1/2 cup finely shredded cheddar cheese

1. In a saucepan over medium to high heat, heat pineapple, including juice until it comes to a boil. Add sugar and stir until dissolved.
2. Add gelatin that has been soaked in cold water. Stir until dissolved, and set in refrigerator to cool. When mixture begins to set, stir in whipped cream, nuts, and cheese.

3. Chill several hours in refrigerator before serving.
4. Can be served in squares atop a bed of lettuce, or in a pretty serving dish.

White Christmas Salad

Makes approximately 12 (4- to 6-ounce) servings
1 large package lemon Jell-O
1/2 pint whipping cream
1 (8-ounce) package cream cheese, crumbled
1 (13 1/2-ounce) can light cherries, drained
1 (13 1/2-ounce) can crushed pineapple, drained
1 small package miniature marshmallows
1 cup chopped pecans

1. In a large bowl or glass baking dish, mix Jell-O according to package instructions. Let stand until slightly syrupy or thickened.
2. Add whipped cream and cream cheese. Let set awhile.
3. Add drained fruit, marshmallows, and pecans. Mix all together and let set in refrigerator.
4. Can be served from a glass baking dish, cut into squares, or from a serving bowl.

Frosted Cranberry Squares

Makes about 9 (4-inch-square) servings.
1 (13 1/2-ounce) can crushed pineapple (1 2/3 cups), drained, liquid reserved
1 (6-ounce) package lemon Jell-O
1 cup ginger ale
1 (1-pound) can jellied cranberry sauce
1 (2-ounce) package of dessert topping (such as Dream Whip)
1 (8-ounce) package cream cheese, softened

green food coloring (optional)
1/2 cup chopped pecans
1 tablespoon butter

1. Add water to reserved pineapple liquid to make 1 cup. Add to a saucepan and heat until boiling. Dissolve Jell-O in hot mixture. Cool and pour into a large bowl.
2. Gently stir ginger ale into Jell-O mixture. Chill until partly set.
3. Meanwhile, in a medium bowl, blend drained pineapple and cranberry sauce. Fold into Jell-O mixture. Turn into a 9-by-9-by-2-inch dish.
4. Prepare dessert topping according to package directions. Fold in softened cream cheese. Add a few drops of green food coloring for a festive Christmas look and mix well. Spread over Jell-O mixture.
5. On a cookie sheet, mix pecans with butter and bake about 10 minutes. Watch carefully to keep them from burning. Sprinkle over top of salad. Chill before serving.

Cranberry Salad

Wonderful as a salad, some even say a dessert, with Thanksgiving and Christmas meals. Serve in a pretty glass bowl.

Makes 10 (4- to 5-ounce) servings.
1 pound fresh cranberries
1 cup sugar
2 cups seedless red grapes, halved
1 cup chopped pecans
1 pint whipping cream, whipped

1. In a food processor, chop cranberries to medium-fine. Pour sugar over cranberries. Cover with foil and let stand overnight.
2. Add grapes, pecans, and whipped cream. Mix well. Keep refrigerated until ready to serve.

Vegetables

Never Out of Style

Mom Reese's Creamed Corn

Makes 10 to 12 (4-ounce) servings
8 to 10 ears of fresh best-quality corn on the cob
1 stick butter
salt and pepper to taste
2 tablespoons sugar
1 cup (or more) half-and-half
1 tablespoon bacon drippings

1. Wash and clean the corn well. With a sharp knife, cut off the kernels about 2/3 the way to the cob. Then, with the back side of your knife, scrape the cob well to capture its natural milk.
2. Put butter in a heavy skillet. Add corn; cook over medium to high heat, stirring constantly. Add salt and pepper to taste and sugar. Add 1 cup half-and-half, more if needed. Add bacon drippings. Cook about 20 minutes.
3. Remove from heat and serve. This recipe also freezes well for future use.

Tip: You can use low-fat milk if you're watching fat content. But otherwise, no shortcuts or substitutions allowed for best results. Yes, you really do need to fry the bacon to get the best bacon drippings!

Baked Scalloped Corn

Makes 8 (5-ounce) servings
1 (15-ounce) can creamed corn
1 (15-ounce) can whole kernel corn
1/4 cup chopped onion

2 eggs, beaten
1/2 cup milk
1 (2-ounce) jar pimento, drained
1/4 cup cracker crumbs
1/4 teaspoon salt
2 tablespoons freshly grated Parmesan cheese
2 tablespoons butter

1. Preheat oven to 350 degrees F. Grease a 9-by-9-inch casserole.
2. In a large bowl, combine all ingredients except for Parmesan and butter, mixing well.
3. Pour in prepared casserole, sprinkle top with Parmesan, and dot with butter.
4. Bake for 40 to 45 minutes. Let stand 5 minutes before serving.

Spinach Artichoke Side Dish

Makes 8 (5-ounce) servings
2 (10-ounce) packages frozen spinach (chopped), thawed and well-drained
1 (6-ounce) jar soft marinated artichoke hearts, drained
2 (3-ounce) packages cream cheese
2 tablespoons butter
1/4 teaspoon pepper
2 tablespoons grated Parmesan cheese

1. Preheat oven to 350 degrees F. Lightly grease a 9-by-9-inch casserole.
2. In a large bowl, combine spinach and artichoke hearts.
3. In a medium bowl, combine cream cheese, butter, and pepper. Stir into spinach mixture.
4. Spoon mixture into prepared casserole. Sprinkle with Parmesan and bake, covered, for 30 minutes. Uncover and bake 10 minutes more.

Aunt Jewell's Pickled Okra

Makes 1 pint
1/2 pound fresh okra
1 bud garlic
1 teaspoon mustard seed
1 teaspoon sugar
3 teaspoons salt
1 cup vinegar

1. Clean fresh okra with a paper towel. Do not wash.
2. Place in a 1-pint canning jar and add garlic, mustard seed, sugar, and salt.
3. In a saucepan, combine vinegar and 1/4 cup water and bring to a boil. Pour over the okra and seal.

Desserts

Always Plentiful in Our Home

Raspberry Cream Dessert

This is a light, pretty, and refreshing dessert, especially when served in individual stemmed glass for a ladies' luncheon or party.

Makes about 10 (4- to 5-ounce) servings
1 (3-ounce) package raspberry-flavored gelatin
1/2 cup boiling water
1 pint vanilla ice cream, softened
1 (10-ounce) package frozen raspberries, thawed
1/2 pint whipping cream, whipped

1. In a large bowl, dissolve gelatin in boiling water.

2. Add ice cream; stir until dissolved, then add raspberries. Refrigerate until set, at least 2 hours.
3. Spoon into serving glasses and return to refrigerator until ready to serve. Add a dollop of whipped cream to each serving.

Four-Layered Chocolate Dessert

Makes 16 (3- to 5-ounce) squares
First layer:
1 cup flour
1/2 cup pecans
1/2 cup melted butter
2 tablespoons powdered sugar

Second layer:

1 (8-ounce) package cream cheese, softened
1 cup powdered sugar
1 cup Cool Whip

Third layer:

3 cups milk
1 teaspoon vanilla
2 small packages instant chocolate pudding

Fourth layer:

2 cups Cool Whip
1/4 cup chopped pecans

1. Preheat oven to 275 degrees F.
2. *Make the first layer:* Mix flour, pecans, butter and sugar. Press into a 9-by-13-inch baking dish. Bake for 15 minutes. Let cool.

3. *Make the second layer:* Mix cream cheese, powdered sugar, and Cool Whip. Spread on top of first layer.
4. *Make the third layer:* Mix milk, vanilla, and chocolate pudding. Spread on top of previous layer.
5. *Make the fourth layer:* Top with Cool Whip and chopped pecans. Refrigerate for several hours before serving.

Frozen Pumpkin Squares

Makes 16 (3- to 4-ounce) servings
2 cups (16-ounce can) pumpkin
1 cup sugar
1 teaspoon cinnamon
1/2 teaspoon nutmeg
1/2 teaspoon salt
1/2 teaspoon ginger
1 cup chopped pecans, toasted
1/2 gallon vanilla ice cream, softened
36 gingersnaps, crushed
whipped cream, for serving
pecan halves, for serving

1. Lightly grease the bottom of a 9-by-13-inch baking dish.
2. In a medium bowl, combine first six ingredients. Add pecans.
3. In a chilled bowl, fold pumpkin mixture into ice cream.
4. Line half of the prepared baking dish with crushed gingersnaps. Top with half the pumpkin mixture. Repeat layers. Freeze until firm, at least five hours.
5. Cut into squares. Garnish with whipped cream and pecan halves.

Aunt Elaine's Strawberry Freeze

Makes 16 (3- to 4-ounce) squares

Crust:

1 cup flour
1/2 cup butter
1/4 cup chopped nuts

Filling:

2 egg whites
1 large package strawberries, partially frozen
1 teaspoon lemon juice
1 teaspoon vanilla
1 cup sugar
1/2 pint whipping cream

1. Preheat oven to 400 degrees F.
2. *Make crust:* In a 9-by-13-inch baking dish, combine flour, butter, and nuts; mix well. Brown in preheated oven 12 to 15 minutes. Cool.
3. *Make filling:* In a large mixing bowl, beat together egg whites and strawberries. Add lemon juice and vanilla. Then gradually add sugar and beat for 20 minutes. (Be sure to beat the full 20 minutes.) Fold in whipped cream.
4. Use a rubber spatula to pour filling into baking dish. Freeze overnight before serving. Store in freezer.

Cherry Dessert

Makes 16 (3- to 4-ounce) servings
2 (15 1/2-ounce) cans cherry pie filling
1 (15-ounce) box white cake mix
1 (15-ounce) can crushed pineapple
1 stick butter, cut into pieces
1 cup fresh coconut flakes

1/2 cup chopped pecans

1. Preheat oven to 325 degrees F. Grease and flour a 9-by-13-inch baking dish.
2. Place cherry pie filling in prepared baking dish. Pour half the cake mix over cherries.
3. Add crushed pineapple with juice and remaining cake mix.
4. Sprinkle butter pieces and then coconut over all. Top with chopped pecans.
5. Bake 50 to 60 minutes. Serve with whipped cream or ice cream.

Christmas Goodies

Over 100 Years of Family Recipes ... and a Few New Ones

Grandma Louise's Pecan Christmas Cake

Makes 2 dozen (2- to 3-ounce) servings

Cake:

1 pound butter
1 cup sugar
6 eggs
1 tablespoon lemon juice
1 teaspoon grated lemon peel
1 tablespoon vanilla
1 pound pecans, coarsely chopped
1 1/2 cups golden raisins
3 cups sifted flour
1/4 teaspoon salt
1 teaspoon baking powder
1/2 cup candied cherries, cut in half

Glaze:

1/4 cup orange juice
1/4 cup lemon juice
1/4 cup sugar

1. Preheat oven to 300 degrees F. Grease a 10-inch tube pan and
    line with parchment paper.

2. *Make cake:* In a large bowl, cream butter and sugar until fluffy. Beat in eggs one at a time. Add lemon juice, lemon peel, and vanilla. Fold nuts, raisins, and dry ingredients into creamed mixture. Finally, add candied cherries. Spoon batter into prepared pan. Bake about 2 hours. Cool, then remove from pan.
3. *Make glaze:* In a saucepan, make a syrup of orange juice, lemon juice, and sugar. Combine and cook until thick and boiling. Pour over cake while glaze is still hot.
4. Once completely cool, cake should be wrapped securely in plastic wrap and then aluminum foil and stored in the refrigerator. Will keep for several weeks.

Tip: All of the following recipes will stay fresh longer if stored in a cool place or refrigerated.

Aunt Vickie's Peanut Butter Fudge

Makes 9 to 10 dozen (1-inch-square) pieces
1 cup sugar
1 cup brown sugar
2 tablespoons butter or margarine
dash salt
1/2 cup evaporated milk
1 cup marshmallows
1/2 cup peanut butter
1 teaspoon vanilla

1. Well-grease a 9-by-13-inch pan.
2. In a saucepan, cook sugars, butter, salt, and milk to a soft ball.
3. Add marshmallows and peanut butter just before removing from heat. Do not stir. Cool to room temperature.
4. Add vanilla. Beat until mixture is creamy, thick, and will hold its shape when dropped from a teaspoon.
5. Pour into prepared pan. Refrigerate at least twenty-four hours, then cut.

Tea Dainties

Makes about 3 dozen cookies
These are perfect for a Christmas tea or coffee, or for children of all ages to satisfy a sweet tooth! You'll need a cookie press to make them.
Makes about 3 dozen cookies
2 sticks butter
2/3 cup sugar
1 egg
2 1/2 cups flour
3/4 teaspoon baking powder
1/2 teaspoon salt
food coloring
vanilla, almond, and lemon extract
powdered sugar, mixed with just enough milk to be of a spreading consistency

1. Preheat oven to 300 to 325 degrees F.
2. In a large bowl, cream softened butter and sugar thoroughly. Add egg and beat well.
3. Sift together flour, baking powder, and salt. Add to the butter mixture with an electric beater. The consistency of the batter will be coarse but suitable for the press.
4. I divide the dough into three batches: one uncolored, flavored with vanilla; one with a few drops of red food coloring, flavored with almond; and one with a few drops of green food coloring, flavored with lemon.
5. Depending on the attachments for your cookie press, you can make Christmas wreaths, trees, poinsettias, and candy canes. (Use the star disc to make the candy cane.)
6. Place on a cookie sheet and bake until just baked, not brown, about 10 minutes or less. Ice with powdered sugar mixture. Use a small paintbrush to put the icing on each cookie. Then use colored sugar sprinkles to decorate.

Note: These freeze well and can be made in advance. Store in the refrigerator or a cool place.

Hazel's Crescent Pecan Cookies

A family favorite.
Makes about 2 dozen cookies
2 sticks butter
2 cups flour
6 tablespoons powdered sugar, plus more for rolling
3 teaspoons vanilla
1/2 pound ground pecans

1. In a large bowl, cream butter. Add remaining ingredients.
2. Shape dough into 1 to 1 1/2-inch crescents. Place on cookie sheet and bake for 13 to 14 minutes.
3. Roll in additional powdered sugar while still warm. May want to roll twice in the powdered sugar.
4. Let cool and store. These cookies freeze well.

Best Sugar Cookies

Makes 3 or 4 dozen
1 cup sugar
1 cup packed powdered sugar
2 sticks butter
1 cup vegetable oil
1/4 teaspoon salt
2 eggs, well beaten
4 cups plus 2 tablespoons flour
1 teaspoon soda
1 teaspoon cream of tartar
1 teaspoon vanilla
colored sugar

1. Preheat oven to 350 degrees F. Lightly grease cookie sheet.
2. In a large bowl, cream sugar, powdered sugar, butter, vegetable oil, and salt.
3. Add eggs and beat well. Sift together flour, soda, and cream of tartar. Add to first mixture. Add vanilla. Chill about thirty minutes.
4. Shape into 1- to 2-inch balls and flatten with the floured bottom of a small juice glass and place on prepared cookie sheet. Sprinkle with colored sugar, if desired.
5. Bake in a 350 degree oven for 10 to 12 minutes or until just slightly browned.

Christmas Cherry Cookies

Makes 2 dozen cookies
1/2 cup butter
1/4 cup sugar
1 egg yolk
1 tablespoon orange rind
1 1/2 teaspoon lemon rind
1 tablespoon lemon juice
1 cup flour
1 egg white
1/2 cup chopped pecans
whole candied cherries

1. Preheat oven to 350 degrees F and lightly grease cookie sheet.
2. In a large bowl, cream butter and sugar. Add egg yolk, orange rind, lemon rind, lemon juice, and flour, in that order. Mix well and chill overnight.
3. Form into 1/2-inch balls. Dip in beaten egg whites and roll in chopped nuts. Place a cherry on top. Place on prepared cookie sheet and bake for 15 to 20 minutes.

Mom Reese's Oatmeal Cookies

These can also have chocolate chips added to them, and they freeze well.

Makes 3 dozen cookies

1 cup sugar

2 sticks butter

2 eggs

1 teaspoon soda

3/4 teaspoon baking powder

2 tablespoons water, divided

1/3 cup buttermilk

2 cups old-fashioned Quaker Oats

2 cups flour, sifted

1/4 teaspoon salt

1 1/2 cups raisins

1. Preheat oven to 375 degrees F. Grease a cookie sheet.
2. In a large bowl, cream sugar and butter. Add eggs and beat well.
3. Dissolve soda and baking powder in a tablespoon of buttermilk. Add to butter mixture, then add remaining buttermilk.
4. In a medium bowl, combine oats, sifted flour, and salt. Add to butter mixture gradually.
5. Heat raisins with a tablespoon of water, then add to butter mixture. Mix well.
6. Drop teaspoon-size balls onto prepared sheet and bake until golden brown, but not hard, about 10 minutes.

Carrot Cookies

Makes about 2 dozen cookies

Cookies:

1 cup shortening or butter
3/4 cup sugar
1 egg
1 teaspoon vanilla
1 teaspoon lemon juice
1 (7 1/2-ounce) jar carrot baby food
2 cups flour
2 teaspoons baking powder
1 teaspoon salt

Icing:

2 cups powdered sugar
1 tablespoon melted butter
3 tablespoons orange juice
1 tablespoon grated orange rind
coconut-flavored and rainbow-mix sprinkles

1. Preheat oven to 375 degrees F. Lightly grease a cookie sheet.
2. *Make cookies:* In a large bowl, cream shortening and sugar. Add egg. Add vanilla, lemon juice, and baby food. Sift flour, baking powder, and salt and combine with first mixture. Mix well. Drop by teaspoonful onto prepared cookie sheet and bake 8 to 10 minutes. Do not allow to brown.
3. *Make icing:* Mix together powdered sugar, melted butter, orange juice, and grated orange rind. Mix well in electric mixer.
4. Ice cookies while still warm and add coconut flavored or rainbow mix sprinkles. Bake just before using; do not freeze.

Acorn Cookies

All-time favorite!
Makes 2 to 3 dozen cookies
1 cup butter
1/2 cup powdered sugar
1 teaspoon vanilla
2 cups flour
1 1/2 teaspoons cooking oil
12 ounces dark chocolate chips
1 1/2 cups finely chopped pecans

1. Preheat oven to 350 degrees F.
2. In a large bowl, cream together butter, powdered sugar, and vanilla. Gradually add flour and mix well.
3. Shape cookies into 1 1/2-inch sticks. Flatten 3/4 inch with a fork. Bake for 12 to 14 minutes. Cool.
4. Place a small pan in a skillet with water over medium to high heat. Add cooking oil to pan and then chocolate chips. Stir chocolate to prevent sticking until it is completely melted.
5. Place about 1 cup of finely chopped pecans in a separate bowl.
6. Dip unflattened tip of cookie in chocolate. Roll the chocolate tip of the cookie in the pecans immediately after dipping. Let cool.
7. Cover tightly and store in a cool place.

Gingerbread Cookies

Makes 3 to 4 dozen (5 1/2-inch) gingerbread men
5 1/2 cups flour
1 teaspoon baking soda
1 teaspoon salt
1 teaspoon cinnamon
1 teaspoon ginger
1 teaspoon cloves

1 teaspoon nutmeg
1 cup shortening
1 cup sugar
1 cup molasses
1 egg
1 teaspoon vanilla

1. Preheat oven to 325 degrees F.
2. In a medium bowl, sift together flour, soda, salt, and spices.
3. In a large bowl, cream shortening and sugar. Beat in molasses, egg, and vanilla. Stir in flour mixture (1/3 at a time), blending well to make a soft dough. Chill 4 hours or overnight.
4. Roll out a quarter of the dough between wax paper to 1/8-inch thickness. Cut with floured cookie cutter. Bake 1 inch apart on ungreased cookie sheet 8 minutes or until firm but not dark. Cool, frost, and decorate.

Aunt Rose's Molasses Christmas Cookies

Makes 3 to 4 dozen cookies
1 cup butter
1/2 cup sugar
1 cup molasses, or 1/2 cup molasses and 1/2 cup honey
3 1/2 cups flour
1 tablespoon ginger
1 tablespoon cinnamon
1 tablespoon nutmeg
1/2 teaspoon ground cloves
1 teaspoon soda dissolved in 3 tablespoons hot water

1. Preheat oven to 325 degrees F.
2. In a large bowl, cream butter and sugar. Add molasses.
3. Sift together flour and spices and add to mixture. Add soda and water mixture. Chill dough in refrigerator.

4. Roll in balls, put on cookie sheet, and flatten with a glass with cloth on it.
5. Place on cookie sheet and bake for 10 to 15 minutes. Let set for a few minutes before removing from sheet.

Cousin Janeyce's Cheese Cake

The Christmas season in our home was not complete if Mother did not make this cheesecake.

Yields 10 (3-ounce) slices
*Crust:*1/2 cup fine graham cracker crumbs
1 tablespoon sugar
1/4 teaspoon cinnamon
1/4 teaspoon nutmeg

Filling:

5 eggs at room temperature, separated
1 cup sugar
1 pound cream cheese, at room temperature
1 cup sour cream
2 tablespoons flour
1 teaspoon vanilla
1 16-ounce can cherry pie filling

1. Heat oven to 275 degrees F.
2. Butter a 10-inch springform pan, sides, and bottom. Dust with a mixture of graham cracker crumbs, sugar, cinnamon and nutmeg.
3. In a large bowl, beat egg yolks until thick and lemon-colored. Gradually beat in sugar. Add softened cream cheese, beating until smooth and creamy. Add sour cream, flour, and vanilla. Continue beating until very smooth.

4. Beat egg whites until stiff but not dry. Gently fold into cream cheese mixture.
5. Pour filling into prepared pan. Bake 70 minutes. Turn oven off but leave in one hour without opening oven door. Remove from oven and cool.
6. Spread cherry pie filling over top of cake.

Christmas Cracker Jacks

Good any time of the year.
Makes approximately 1 pound
2 cups brown sugar, firmly packed
1/2 cup light or dark syrup
1 stick margarine
pinch of cream of tarter
1 teaspoon soda
5 quarts freshly popped corn

1. Preheat oven to 300 degrees F. Lightly grease 2 cookie sheets.
2. In a saucepan, boil sugar, syrup, margarine, and cream of tartar for 5 minutes. Stir in soda.
3. In a large bowl, mix sugar mixture thoroughly with popped corn. Spread on prepared cookie sheets.
4. Bake for 40 minutes, stirring every 10 minutes.

Sugared Nuts

Makes 1 pound
1 cup brown sugar packed
1/2 cup white sugar
1/2 cup sour cream
1 teaspoon vanilla
1 pound English walnuts or pecans (or both)

1. In a heavy saucepan, combine sugars and sour cream. Cook over medium heat, without stirring, until a little of the mixture dropped in cold water forms a soft ball. Remove from heat.
2. Stir in nuts. Pour onto wax paper. With a fork, separate nuts. Let dry completely.

Aunt Rose's Chocolate-Covered Peanuts

Makes 4 dozen one-inch clusters.
1 teaspoon vegetable or olive oil
12 to 15 ounces dark chocolate chips
1 (16-ounce) jar Planter's peanuts (salted, unsalted, or dry roasted)

1. Put a teaspoon of cooking oil in a heavy saucepan and add chocolate chips. Melt the chocolate morsels over hot water. Stir with a wooden spoon until the chocolate chips are completely melted and smooth. No lumps.
2. Remove from heat and add the peanuts. Stir well with a wooden spoon.
3. With a small spoon, place peanuts on waxed paper in the size of your choice. I make them rather small because they are rich. Teaspoon-size drops will yield two to three dozen. Adjust amounts of chocolate chips and peanuts according to your desired yield.

Note: You can use a double boiler to melt the chocolate or put it in a heavy saucepan and place the pan in a cast iron skillet over medium high heat.

Festive Punch

For Christmas holidays or any special occasion. Easy and so good!
Makes approximately 25 (6-ounce) servings

1 (46-ounce) can pineapple juice
1 (12-ounce) can frozen orange juice
1 (12-ounce) can frozen lemonade
1 (2-liter) bottle ginger ale

Mix together slightly ahead of when you want to serve so the frozen juices can thaw.

Note: You can add a package of Kool-Aid to make it a desired color.

CPSIA information can be obtained
at www.ICGtesting.com
Printed in the USA
BVHW080805030121
596864BV00013B/493